Lead Then Learn

Lead Then Learn

Powering Project Teams With Collaboration

Annie MacLeod, PMP

BEP

BUSINESS EXPERT PRESS

Leader in applied, concise business books

First published in 2024 by
Business Expert Press, LLC
222 East 46th Street, New York, NY 10017
www.businessexpertpress.com

ISBN-13: 978-1-63742-579-4 (paperback)
ISBN-13: 978-1-63742-580-0 (e-book)

Business Expert Press Portfolio and Project Management Collection

First edition: 2024

10 9 8 7 6 5 4 3 2 1

This book is dedicated to those who came before—all my mentors—
Bob, Francis and Ethel and to those who inspire me for the future—
Kate, Clare, and Kathleen

Description

Whether you are a project manager just starting your career or a seasoned expert trying to introduce more collaboration into your organization, this book is for you! In this practical guide, full of templates and techniques for every type of project and at any stage, we'll give you ways to reduce the chaos of a startup and improve your project team's morale.

I'll help you build and sustain high-performing teams, add visual collaboration to your project management toolkit, get the most out of not just your team but also your vendors and contractors, and ensure that you have delighted customers to receive all the results of the team's great work.

Starting with project initiation and moving through planning, executing, adapting, and ultimately closing and reflecting on the project are all covered. In addition, all these phases will be supplemented with ways to gather input from your team, get feedback on team performance, and continuously improve project processes in your organization all the while keeping a project on track with time, scope, and budget expectations.

All these tools and techniques are tailored to be used with Miro, the leading collaboration tool available. You can utilize these techniques wherever you are in your project by jumping into sections that apply and appeal to you and your team.

Keywords

collaboration tools for project managers; project management for beginners; project teams; project teamwork; project communication; project coordination; collaborative decision making

Contents

Testimonials

"Annie does a masterful job of illustrating how to foster team collaboration within real-world project management environments. Newly-minted project managers and those who want to up their collaboration practices will walk away with advice and techniques they can put into practice right away." —**Galen Low, Cofounder, The Digital Project Manager**

"An impactful tool for project teams striving for success. Annie guides with practical workshops and activities for each project stage, equipped with meticulously crafted agendas and templates, ensuring meetings are purposeful, engaging, and yield results."—**Eleanor Hooker, Head of Community, Miro**

"I can see this sitting on my desk and me flipping to various topics as I hit that point in a project. It's a terrific guide through the whole process and I think the Project Management GameBoard concept and graphics really help ground you in the whole process in a necessary way."—**Kim White, Senior Consultant, Rali**

*"*Lead Then Learn *is a must-have resource for project managers of all levels. This book offers unique and valuable tools to easily navigate every stage of a project. With Annie MacLeod's insight that 'Collaboration is not about who is the loudest person in the room,' the book highlights the importance of effective teamwork.* Lead Then Learn *sets itself apart by emphasizing the value of all stakeholders' input in a collaborative environment that project managers co-create with their teams."*—**Barbara Kephart, PMP, Founder, Projects Pivot Inc.**

Acknowledgments

This book would not have been possible without the help of many people. First, my project management mentors, Gary James, Dr. Francis Hartman, and Bob Gerst. Jon White and Cindy Pupp, thanks for cheering me on throughout this journey and always being generous with your time and listening to my brain dumps. To Mel Clifford and Trent Janisch who worked with me to develop the original analog version of the Project Management GameBoard. Thanks to Kam Jugdev for encouraging me to not just write this book but also take on a new vocation and acquire new skills! All these people taught me a great deal and helped lay the groundwork to make this book possible.

I had a great team of peer review resources who spent significant time reviewing a draft and gave thoughtful feedback that was critical to creating a more polished manuscript. Thanks to Cindy Pupp, Shane Spraggs, Jon White, and Kim White.

Thanks also go to many clients I've had the opportunity to work with, particularly in the last three years, to solidify my thinking on key aspects of the Project Management GameBoard.

Finally, thanks to Miro for building such an amazing collaboration platform that allowed me to take my clunky facilitation tool kit (Figure A.1) into the 21st century and the virtual world.

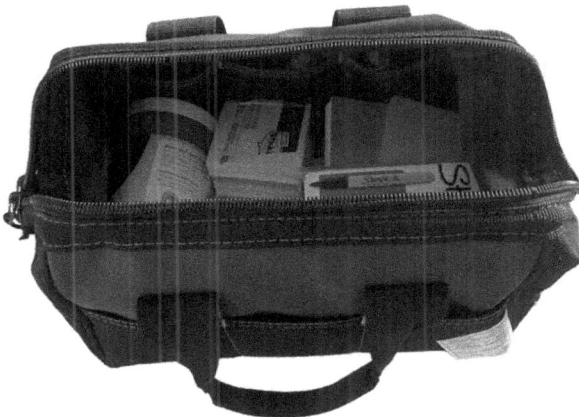

Figure A.1 Facilitation tool kit

CHAPTER 1

Introduction

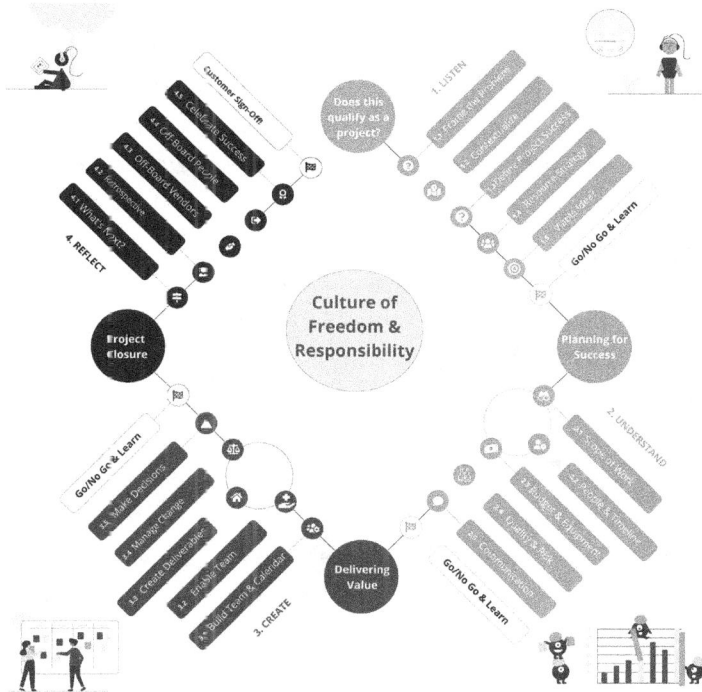

Figure 1.1 The Project Management GameBoard

Background

Welcome to *Lead Then Learn, Powering Project Teams With Collaboration*! This book is born out of almost 40 years of project management experience, primarily in what would be described as the tech sector. It is anchored or presented through the model of the Project Management GameBoard (PMGB); see Figure 1.1. The PMGB is a great way to present all the tools, techniques, and templates I've built over this career.

Later in my career, I had the opportunity to coach and mentor project managers (PMs), starting at the City of Calgary in the early 2000s. This has become my passion and is a key reason for this book—this is my legacy piece to share with the project management community in the hope it helps PMs and others in a PM role but perhaps not that title.

Intended Audience

One of the things I truly enjoy about project management are the people who are attracted to it, the background they come from, the skills or specializations they have, and where their passions are. It is one of the few careers that are open to so much diversity of backgrounds, disciplines, and aspirations. There is always more to learn, try, and interest a person about projects and project management.

All that said, this book is intended for or targeted at folks who are early in their careers—probably already a PM or a business analyst. Even if you aren't called a PM, it may be in your duties. I often call these folks voluntold PMs!

You may be a PM who aspires to bring new collaboration techniques into your tool belt or to diversify your portfolio of projects by expanding your facilitation abilities to break into a new industry.

In the case of business analysts, you are probably looking to build your collaboration chops and supplement them with some PM best practices.

Finally, this book may be of benefit to C-suite types who are looking to bring order to chaos—those startup organizations now moving to their next revenue goal. They are typically big enough to warrant some project management discipline but not particularly suited to a pure Agile approach—those in product development or services. They can also be more mature organizations looking to add collaborative practices into their project teams to enhance employee attraction and retention.

If any of that's true, then you've come to the right place!

Purpose

This book and the PMGB are an encapsulation of what I think are best practices for project teams that want to harness collaboration to make their projects and their project teams successful. I'm very passionate about collaboration as I've seen it done well and power project teams to success and I've frequently seen it done poorly.

Collaboration is also very topical. I constantly hear or read articles asking why different levels of government, different organizations, and different departments within organizations can't collaborate more or better. The simple answer is that it's *hard*! As many of us know, particularly anyone who was thrown into a group work project at school or university, it doesn't happen easily! This book is intended to showcase visual tools and techniques that can be applied throughout a project life cycle to truly collaborate.

On top of collaboration a foundational aspect of the PMGB is the difference between processes and projects. I've found that many organizations, particularly digital-based ones, call everything a project when they are delivering projects to customers but should be managing them as processes. There is a fundamental difference that is represented by the process performance triangle (Figure 1.2).

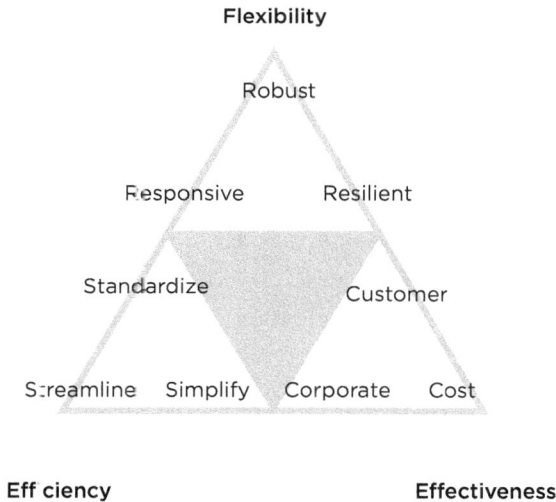

Flexibility

Robust

Responsive   Resilient

Standardize   Customer

Streamline   Simplify   Corporate   Cost

Eff ciency   **Effectiveness**

Figure 1.2 Process performance triangle

When managing processes, we need to understand the performance along three attributes:

- *Efficient*: standardize, streamline, and simplify
- *Effective*: customer, cost, and corporate
- *Flexible*: responsive, resilient, and robust

When we treat processes as projects, we miss out on some key opportunities to improve our ability to deliver to customers and optimize performance to meet corporate goals.

The PMGB provides a model for project management with a light touch, and then each step within each leg of the board provides you with collaboration tools and techniques to try. The intent is not to go step by step, by step linearly through the board—this is impossible—as every project, every organization, and every team is a little bit different. The intent is to find where you are in your project and then select the tools and techniques that best suit what you are trying to achieve in your project or with your team.

In 2018, I was introduced to Miro (www.miro.com/about/), an online workspace and collaboration tool. This technology has allowed me to templatize many of the workshops that I've run and provides the platform for the digital PMGB.

It provides a way for project teams to visualize their project and facilitate key project activities. Visualization is the secret sauce for making these experiences powerful in project teams. In our complex project world, it makes information more accessible and easier to absorb for every project stakeholder and for the project team to collaborate. Research by 3M found that we can process information visually 60,000 times faster than text (www.shiftelearning.com/blog/bid/350326/studies-confirm-the-power-of-visuals-in-elearning).

Just take the example in Figure 1.3.

You can already see why visualization is so powerful!

Graphic Description	Textual Description
	*A plane figure with four equal straight sides and four right angles.*

Figure 1.3 Visualization

Now think about a project status report as a visual image; compare these two and think about which could be more effective (Figure 1.4 versus Figure 1.5).

See my point?!?

Status Report: 12/10/20 - 19/10/20

Job Details

Client & Brand	Aston Baby	AM	Ben Aston
Job Name & Number	ABY 2342 - Baby Walking Shoes Landing Page	PM	Hannah McNamee
Client Contact	Rebecca Miller - rebecca@astonbaby.com / 604.776.4587		

Executive Summary

Schedule	Live date is delayed by one week to 24th November due to image asset delays. This may move further depending on when they are supplied.
Budget	OK - Third party assets were more expensive than anticipated but overall budget remains healthy.
Scope	Depending on the feedback from v5 of the of the copy - a Change Request may be required for additional work.

Progress Summary

Completed This Week	Planned For Next Week
- All wireframes and layout variants were completed, and v2 was approved.	- Finalise copy adapts and get approval for all copy
- Content refinement, to develop v5 of the copy.	- Complete design rollout + presentation
- Design concepts were presented and approved	- Complete technical setup

Action Items

Aston Baby	Owner	Due Date	Resolved	Notes
Provide feedback to v5 copy edits	Rebecca	20/10/18	-	Delay is impacting the

Figure 1.4 Text-based project status report

Organization

The book is organized by the four legs of the PMGB, with a chapter dedicated to each:

- *Listen*: qualifying our ideas—project initiation
- *Understand*: planning for success—project planning
- *Create*: delivering value—project execution
- *Reflect*: learning and celebrating—project close and retrospectives

This way, you can dive into the content specific to your current project and where it's at. You'll also notice that at the end of each leg is a

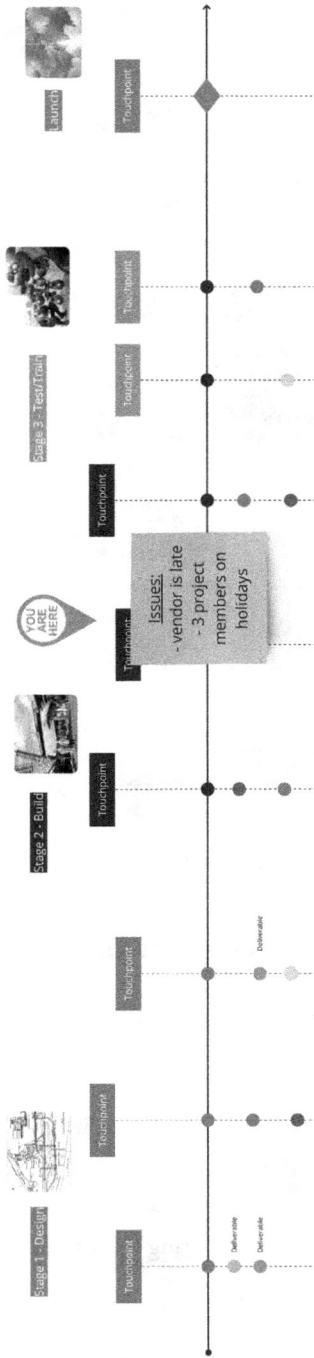

Figure 1.5 Visual project status report

Figure 1.6 Go/No Go & Learn

checkered flag, which represents a decision point: Go/No Go for each leg (Figure 1.6).

These flags are project gates or milestones or off-ramps, an opportunity for the project to come up for air, look around, and review its progress as well as the conditions outside of the project. This provides a way to put a project on hold without losing the effort that has gone into developing it so far. If priorities or circumstances change—as they so often do—we can put the project on hold neatly and cleanly.

The book provides you with examples of workshops and activities at each stage of a project. Each workshop will typically include a proposed agenda and template(s) for the associated activities. These tools are invaluable to ensure you have meetings that are well thought out, engaging, achieve results, and ensure the attendees can provide their input and are respectful of their time. The agenda will be in the format of:

Purpose: Why are we having this meeting/workshop?
Process: What is the process we will use to accomplish the meeting/workshop? This pays particular attention to activities in the workshop.
Payoff: What is the desired outcome for our meeting/workshop?

The other key piece of this book is the online resources that are available to supplement the book content. For electronic readers, we've got links to multiple resources and references. Through the PMGB website (www.pmgameboard.com), readers are also able to access templates referenced in the book.

While I would be honored if you read the book from cover to cover, I would encourage you to use it as a resource for when you're stuck or want to freshen up some practices in your project. If your project is underway, find the leg best related to the stage you're at and explore some techniques to improve your success. If you're looking to specifically upgrade your team collaboration, then start from the last chapter and select some collaboration techniques to try, regardless of where your project is at—just customize them to suit your project!

Happy collaborating!

CHAPTER 2

Listen—Qualifying Our Ideas

This leg of the PMGB is focused on qualifying our ideas, hence the term Listen—this is not about who shouts the loudest or who's doing the shouting! It is about ensuring we have a viable project. It encompasses touching all the bases to begin to understand the broad aspects of the potential scope, timing, and resource commitment before taking the next steps. This stage is also about getting basic information so that multiple projects can be assessed and prioritized relative to each other.

It's important to remember that this leg of the Project Management GameBoard applies to both client-initiated projects (ones that are processes for our organization) and ideas that may create projects for our organization. We need to complete each step in this leg; however, the emphasis and details will vary.

There is never enough capacity for an organization to undertake every idea that is generated; therefore, the ideas need to be consistently evaluated to ensure we focus on those that will get the most "bang for the buck" as opposed to those that are great ideas but not feasible or the timing is bad. The steps in this leg ensure that we avoid shiny penny syndrome—so often a senior executive spots a new piece of technology and decides "We gotta have that" and it turns out to be a solution looking for a problem!

For client projects, we need to ensure that our client has set this project up for success within their organization, so this leg will be about answering those key questions to ensure they have the capacity, resources, and organizational alignment to make the project successful.

Finally, this leg of the board is primarily "owned" by senior executives in the organization—as the owners of the corporate key performance indicators and strategic plan. It is in the Understand leg where the ownership moves to the project manager (PM) and the project team.

This leg starts with getting on the board; so, we'll start there and then move into the five steps in this leg. The intent is for you to touch each step and then, depending on the organization's project maturity, skills in project management, and strategic and process management, to go as deep as necessary in each step. The analogy is to touch every base and then ensure that you make a collaborative decision at the endpoint: the Go/No Go and Learn checkpoint. We need everyone to be aligned at the end of each leg—within the project and in the broader organization.

Taking an idea and making it into a project!

Figure 2.1 PMGB Listen

For the Listen leg as illustrated in Figure 2.1, we have the following steps:

- Does this qualify as a project? Getting on the board!
- 1.1 Frame the Problem: What are we trying to fix?
- 1.2 Contextualize: How does this "fit" with the organizational priorities and other competing projects? How would/could this impact our customers?

- 1.3 Define Project Success: What and who will make this project successful?
- 1.4 Resource Strategy: What is our strategy to provide resources for this project?
- 1.5 Viable Idea: Bringing all the above together to decide its viability.
- Go/No Go and Learn: Are we ready to go to the next leg—Understand? What have we learned that will improve our project intake going forward?

Does This Qualify as a Project?

Getting on the Board

Does this qualify as a project?

Figure 2.2 PMGB getting on the board

As you can see at the top of this leg, we determine whether this is a project (Figure 2.2). This provides a place to start and it especially brings up the critical conversation about how your organization defines a project. My clients seem to lean toward two extremes: They treat everything as a project or nothing as a project. This makes defining what a project is in your organization particularly important!

Defining how your organization decides what a project is also has the benefit of reducing the likelihood you will boil the ocean! I've seen so many organizations take on too many projects at once and then not successfully achieve or complete them and realize the value that was intended. It's not just about doing the project right, but about doing the right project. Defining a project and completing the Listen leg will make sure you're selecting the right projects with the most likelihood of success.

Project Management Institute (PMI) defines a project as:

a temporary endeavor undertaken to create a unique product service or result

Let's take this and break it down a bit:

- *Temporary*—It has a beginning and an end.
- *Unique*—This is the tricky part: What does unique mean to your organization?
- *Service or result*—This typically means an outcome. Ideally that outcome is a measurable improvement in a process.

So, I recommend that organizations be clear on how they define uniqueness in their organization, paying particular attention to their customers. For example, if a company builds shopping malls—which is their core line of business—are these truly projects? I would argue no—they are projects to their customers but not to their organization.

This is important because if you are treating building shopping malls as projects, then you may be measuring success by the parameters of time, scope, and budget when you should be measuring success by effectiveness, efficiency, and flexibility. Also, it's important to recognize the difference to ensure you spend time with the customer to truly understand the key aspects of the project from their perspective—not just what your organization typically delivers.

Other considerations I've seen in organizations are measures of the project size and complexity. For example, how many departments does it engage, or is the budget at least $xxxk? When the organization has a definition of what a project is and consistently applies that definition, it will help facilitate a conversation when comparing multiple projects to select which ones to proceed—be resourced—and which ones may need to wait.

1.1 Frame the Problem

Now that we know we have a project, we start with framing the problem: It is essential that projects are initiated to solve problems, so we need to frame the problem. This can be as simple as a good problem statement or as complex as an intense series of workshops to clearly articulate the problem you're trying to solve. Regardless of the size of your organization or the maturity of your project management processes, this is a must-have to complete this leg.

For a good problem statement, the resources provided by Six Sigma are great! Check out www.6sigma.us/problem-statement/effective-problem-solving-with-a-problem-statement/#:~:text=A%20good%20problem%20statement%20should%20be%3A,convey%20directly%20to%20the%20reader. There is also a template in Miro to "pitch" your project that includes some expanded questions to complete your problem statement (www.miro.com/miroverse/project-pitch/). Once you've completed this work, it will be one of the elements reviewed in 1.5 Viable Idea as well as Go/No Go and Learn.

Finally, when initiating a client project, you will go through the same step using the same resources—having the client clearly articulate the problem that your solution is anticipated to resolve. This is particularly important for service organizations as your solution may be standardized but each client may customize that solution or feel it addresses a different need in their organization that you may have not anticipated.

1.2 Contextualize

Contextualizing your project means whether you understand the environment that the project will operate within. Again, remember what we've said previously that projects are competing for scarce resources while juggling operational demands and other concurrent projects. There may even be other projects or initiatives going on that could either complement or compete with this initiative. This is where we look around the horizon of the organization to see what these are.

If there are existing corporate documents, methods, and reporting, you want to utilize them wherever possible. If these don't exist, you may need to build them or, at the very least, put more time into the Listen leg to ensure your project gets started on the right foot.

I've found that two key resources are often available to help contextualize projects. These are:

- Strategic plans and/or objectives and key results (OKRs)
- Customer journey maps

These are great methods to contextualize project ideas and help us build the other steps in this leg of the board as well as inform the Understand leg when we plan details of our project.

Leveraging OKRs and Strategic Plan

Many organizations today utilize OKRs or strategic plans to align the organization, define measurable goals, and track outcomes (www.en .wikipedia.org/wiki/Objectives_and_key_results). OKRs are great for defining the vision of the organization and how objectives or strategies will contribute to achieving the corporate vision; these are a natural starting point for kicking off projects or informing your project initiation. Key results (KRs) are the measures of those objectives—how we know they have been realized—ideally in a quantifiable form.

It is not my intent to go into a treatise on OKRs or strategic planning; suffice it to say that these are great sources of information to contextualize projects when they are being initiated. Key things to look for are:

- Understanding how your project idea contributes to specific objectives can help ensure you get the resources you need in terms of people and money. In most organizations, people are measured and rewarded or compensated based on their objectives; this provides a real incentive to ensure their success and in turn your project's success. These folks are great sponsors for your project.
- Be aware that if your project idea doesn't align with any corporate objectives, then it may mean it is a "pet" project and you, as a PM, may struggle to get interdepartmental resources and budgets. These "pet" projects often have passionate sponsors or champions who don't have the authority to marshal the resources—financial and otherwise—that you'll need. As a PM who often has limited authority in an organization, you'll have even less ability to acquire those resources.
- OKRs and strategic planning documents can give you either quantifiable or qualitative information to develop your project

success criteria (step 1.3); otherwise, you'll need to build these specifically for your project.

- Finally these documents may also provide insights into your problem statement that we just created in step 1.1 Frame the Problem; so, be sure to go back and revisit that in case you can further refine it or add more clarity.

There are multiple ways to use this information. I would recommend you either:

- Use it to frame a workshop you'll do in step 1.3 to Define Project Success.
- Inform the discussion about whether this is a viable idea in step 1.5.
- And/or as part of the Go/No Go decision after this leg. More on that later!

Customer Journey Maps

This is a tool that has come out of the Lean world and is meant to visually represent the customer's journey from finding a customer to fulfilling their need and maintaining the relationship. I've found this an invaluable tool to better understand organization structures that are often obtuse: What do all those org chart titles mean, other than some type of pecking order?

Customer journey maps can provide key information when initiating projects:

- They put customers first and can provide insights into customer sentiment: Where do customers need or want improvements?
- They provide insights into corporate processes: How are they performing in terms of efficiency, effectiveness, and flexibility? What are the key customer value adds and key hand-offs in the process?
- These maps also don't suffer from the blind spots that corporate org charts do. If you are a flat organization or

operate in teams as opposed to hierarchies, these are a great tool to visualize where and which teams fit in.

- What are the key systems our project could affect?

I have used it so often and rarely found an organization that truly had a comprehensive customer journey map; so, my colleague Jonathan White of Improve Consulting Services and I developed a template to use in any for-profit organization (Figure 2.3).

There is a PDF version of this template available at www.pmgameboard.com/product/customer-journey-map-template/. With this template, you can capture key information to ensure your project is initiated as comprehensively as possible. Note that it is very rare for an organization to have all this information at its fingertips or even at all. However, this template provides you with a place to capture and visualize what you do have.

Some of the key parts of the template are:

- Horizontal columns: These are the three stages of the customer life cycle—acquire customers, fulfill sales, and retain customers. Every organization goes through these three to a greater or lesser degree. I usually start completing this section by referring to the departments in the corporate org chart and the leadership team. Don't be surprised if there is no alignment between your corporate departments and these phases—do the best you can.
- Journey steps: This is where you can customize the terminology for the columns to a language specific to your organization. The questions under each column will help guide you to complete the bolded descriptor, which is typically a department or group within a department.
- Process/action: Again customize to your organization— identify what steps add value to the organization and especially to the customer.
- Key performance indicators: These are the measures that tell us how that process is performing. Typical measures will be quality, cost, and cycle time.
- "How is this working for our customer/clients?" This is another type of indicator—of how customers feel about

Figure 2.3 Customer journey template

this part of the process. While some organizations have sophisticated customer metrics or feedback measurements, at a minimum, you can capture this from your stakeholders if these aren't quantified in your organization.

- Process ownership: Ideally in your organization there is one person responsible for each step—not a committee; as they say, whose neck do you choke when this isn't working—it's all about accountability. If you're not sure what a process owner role entails, here's some further definition:

> This resource is responsible for the day-to-day operational activities within their department and the data flow through their department. This responsibility includes ensuring that their operational performance is effective, efficient, and flexible to meet customer and corporate requirements. They are responsible to develop and report on that performance to their operational team as well as the organization overall. In a project, they identify opportunities for improvement, provide guidance on the implementation of new processes/technology, and ensure their staff is trained. They are responsible for ensuring that new processes/technology are embedded into the department and realize the benefits.

- *Resources*: These are the people that support the process owner; often this may be the department they work in, but as more organizations move to team structures and utilize partners and external vendors, it is important to consider all these people in the resources section.
- *Systems*: This section allows you to identify at a high level the systems that support each part of the process. As many systems have a "core" function, they perform well and should more readily align with your stages of the customer life cycle or process steps. It is critical to understand your technology footprint as your project will probably need to integrate, modify, or work around it.

Contextualizing your project is all about leveraging as much existing corporate documentation as is available. This will prevent project teams from:

- Repeating work already done in other corporate planning activities
- Reinventing models just to suit their project

Note that when you are doing a client project, this step will have a light touch—typically what would be clarified is any project dependencies your client has with other initiatives in their organization.

1.3 Define Project Success

I've found this step to be critical whether you are truly delivering a project (a unique activity to your organization) or repeatedly delivering projects to customers (a process to us but a project to the client). This step can ensure we understand upfront:

- What the result of the project is expected to look like.
- Why the client undertook this project—this can uncover a whole bunch of critical information about why our sales pitch was successful in the first place and ensure we don't make assumptions about the client.
- Perspectives of key stakeholders and ensure they are aligned.

There are two key tools or collaborative methods to uncover this information that we'll review in detail: the project priority triangle and project success criteria.

Project Priority Triangle Reimagined

The traditional project priority triangle has three points: time, scope, and budget; and PMs are supposed to balance all three. I've found that you actually get only two and it's best represented by Figure 2.4.

Minimize Time   **Maximize Scope**

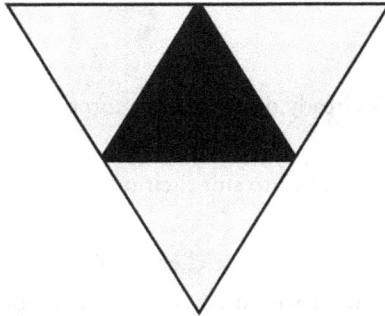

Minimize Cost

Figure 2.4 Project priority triangle

It is often referred to as the balance between time, scope, and cost but it's about fast, cheap, and good! How quickly do we need to go, how much money do we have to spend, and how well do we understand what's needed?

The triangle at this stage of the project is used to understand the priorities or emphasis—pick any two or the easier question—which one are you willing to sacrifice to achieve the other two?

The reason we do this upfront is that it has some downstream implications:

- If we want to minimize time, there are implications for both scope and budget—going quickly precludes maximizing scope.
- If we want to minimize cost, there are implications for both time and scope—time is money and scope can't be maximized but needs to be very specific to keep the project on budget.
- If we have flexibility on scope and time, then when we do project planning in the Understand leg, we'll want to have ranges for the budget instead of one fixed number.
- When (not if) we have project changes identified in the Create (implementation) leg of the project, we can assess these based on the initial project priorities to ensure we continue to align with stakeholder expectations.

It's important to note that PMI has also brought these same concepts into the seventh edition of the *Project Management Body of Knowledge* (*PMBoK*). They talk about projects using approaches of predictive, hybrid, and adaptive. Predictive and hybrid projects develop their own cadence—this would be particularly true when you have an unclear scope. In time-based projects, you'd want to adopt a more predictive system of stage gates or milestones to achieve the intended outcomes.

Let's explore three scenarios to illustrate the impact of different projects on the project priority triangle.

Scenario 1: Minimize Time, Maximize Scope— We Will Spend Money to Ensure We Meet Our Scope and Timeline

- *Minimize time*: This is straightforward—if there is any kind of deadline, this needs to be the top priority. Think about whether your project is tied to a construction season, product launch, or other types of seasonality; these will mean that your project is anchored to minimizing time. This is also the best axis to start the conversation with because then you can determine what the negotiation piece is, for the other two variables.

- *Maximizing scope*: There are two ways to think of scope— in terms of the specification and tolerance or variation to the specification. Think of the difference between pouring concrete, which has an exacting specification and the ability to test to that specification, and building a software interface. An exacting specification would usually occur in a detailed scientific configuration; this would have characteristics of precise measurements and probably 3D schematics for the build. This would also mean that the customer of the project is very knowledgeable and could provide detailed specifications.

  The contrast would be an inexact scope—often Agile or system projects are not specific in their design, especially early on; these types of projects are often initiated to solve

a problem where the solution to the problem is not known
or where the solution could have multiple facets to it that
require testing and iteration. This will mean that beauty is in
the eye of the beholder. I'm afraid I get to harp on it again—
another reason why it's so important to understand who your
customer is!

The next attribute of scope is the tolerance for variation
to the specification. Again, if we are building a scientific
piece of equipment, the tolerance would/could be very
low for variation; this type of equipment is built to an
exacting standard and will be unacceptable if the standard
is not met. This is also true of concrete: It either works or
it doesn't!

- *Cost*: We know intuitively that to hit a fixed date and maximize
  the scope, we'll need to spend money, so in this scenario, we'll
  spend money to achieve these priorities. This is critical to
  understand at these early stages of the project so that when we
  work on the Understand leg and develop our project budget,
  we have range estimates of what the project will cost.

The triangle looks like Figure 2.5.

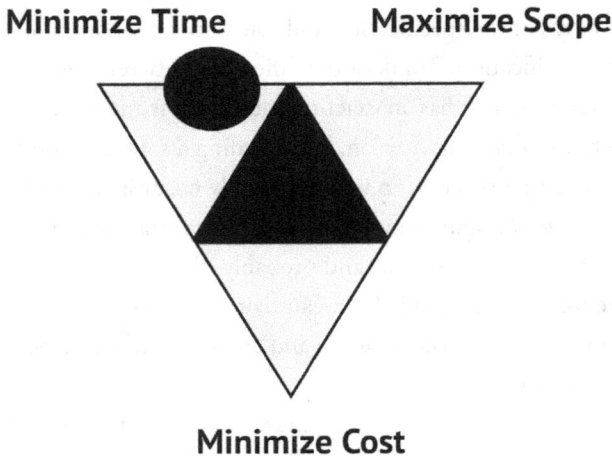

Minimize Time   **Maximize Scope**

Minimize Cost

**We will spend money to ensure we meet our scope
and timeline**

Figure 2.5 PPT scenario 1

Scenario 2: Minimize Cost, Maximize Scope, We Will Take the Time Within Our Limited Budget to Achieve This Specific Scope

This scenario is almost an oxymoron because we know that time is money; however, it can occur when we have a fixed budget that probably only reflects external costs for a project that heavily utilizes uncosted internal resources that are working part-time on the project.

Maximize scope: As you know from our discussion previously, this project will require an exacting scope—we will know what the scope is upfront. Also, this will require a strong relationship with the customer or client of the project to ensure there is neither ambiguity nor clear expectations.

Minimize cost: This is a project that will only incur minimal external costs; therefore, we will have clear sight of the external vendors or suppliers we are dealing with—they will be in existing relationships with us and strong partners.

Time: This is the variable we have for this project—we'll take as long as it takes.

The triangle looks like Figure 2.6.

Minimize Time   **Maximize Scope**

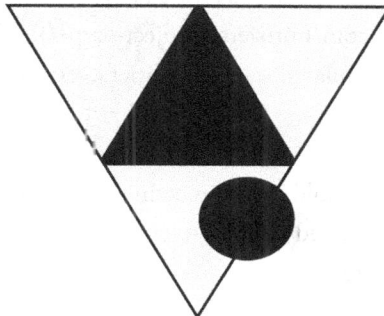

Minimize Cost

We will take the time within our limited budget to achieve this specific scope

Figure 2.6 PPT scenario 2

Overall, I've found this scenario works well for projects that have a defined urgent problem—a specific piece of software functionality needs to be changed or enhanced to meet an urgent business driver such as a new product launch—and often results in multiple phases to the project to meet requirements not originally identified in the scope.

Scenario 3: Minimize Time, Minimize Cost—We Will Sacrifice Scope to Meet Our Timeline and Budget

This is the scenario that I often find project teams are in without realizing it, and that's why I advocate getting it clear upfront!

Minimize time: As we spoke about earlier, there is probably a fixed date or key corporate requirement that needs to be met.

Minimize cost: This is typically the second priority when the budget is tight—so typically in most organizations for most projects.

Scope: If you don't have an exact specification or detailed requirements, and especially if you don't have a really clear problem definition and context of the problem, this is where this set of project priorities can go wrong and the project team will be set up for failure.

Your project priority triangle will look like Figure 2.7.

To facilitate the development of the project priority triangle with your stakeholders, there is a template. It's located in the Miroverse as the Scope Template (www.miro.com/miroverse/project-scope/). There is detailed instruction with the template; however, a brief overview of how this is to be facilitated is:

- Invite all the stakeholders to a meeting (those that would benefit or be impacted by the project).
- Present your materials from steps 1.1 Framing the Problem and 1.2 Contextualizing the Project.
- Solicit their input on each priority individually.
- Consolidate the input by looking for commonalities.
- Have the group reach a consensus on the overall priority for the project.

Minimize Time   Maximize Scope

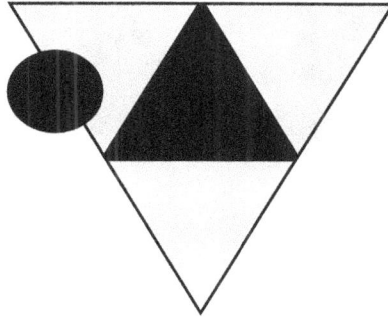

Minimize Cost

We will sacrifice scope to meet our timeline and budget

Figure 2.7 PPT scenario 3

This is a key artifact throughout the project, so keep it handy as we're going to be referring to it not only in the Understand leg but also in the Create leg when we are implementing the project. It is part of our vision or North Star and if it changes or waivers, we need to know why and communicate those changes and any affected decisions or implications.

Success Criteria and Who, Won, and Done

Developing the project priority triangle is an easy segue into developing project success criteria. We can take the stakeholder input from the project priority triangle exercise and build them into success criteria and then into who, won, and done (Figure 2.8). There is a Miro version of this template available at www.miro.com/miroverse/project-scope/.

Success criteria are the next level of detail in defining the project and will provide us with qualitative information that allows us to better understand the scope of the project, particularly from the viewpoint of our key stakeholders.

Who, won, and done are adapted from Dr. Francis Hartman's book *Don't Park Your Brain Outside* (www.amazon.ca/Dont-Park-Brain-Outside-

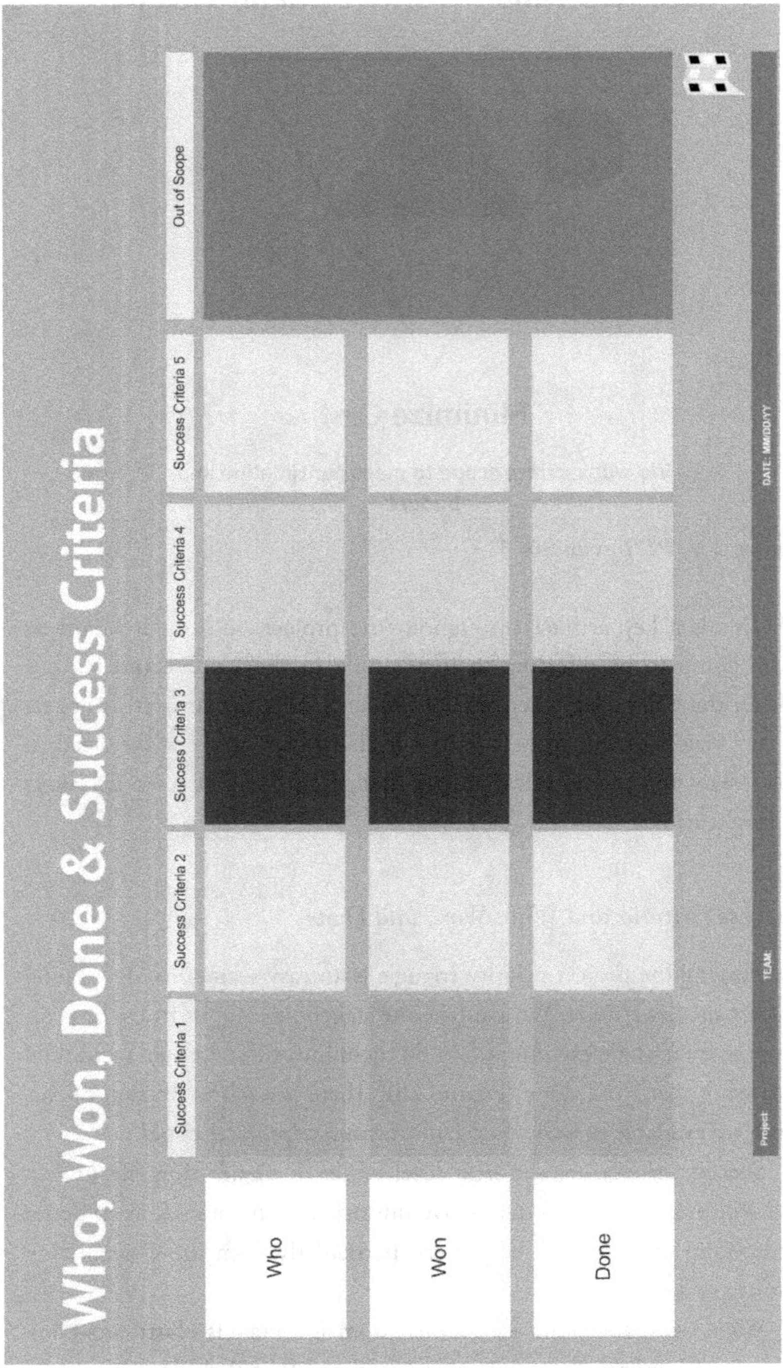

Figure 2.8 Who, won, done & success criteria template

R-T/dp/1880410486). These take our success criteria and add another level of specificity to further understand our scope.

These exercises are especially important to understand whether the idea or problem identified so far has the support and clarity required to proceed. By having these done in a collaborative workshop, it ensures a couple of things:

- Key stakeholders all have input.
- Stakeholders hear each other's perspectives on the problem or proposed solution.
- You get alignment within the senior levels of the organization as early as possible; these are the folks who will provide the people, budgetary, and other resources for your project.
- The team that develops the project plan has the clarity of executive expectations. This transition from executive vision to project team planning is a common downfall of many projects.

To complete this exercise, you may want to carry on from the workshop used to develop the project priority triangle or reconvene a new workshop. Again, we've provided a template at Miroverse—Project Scope (www.miro.com/miroverse/project-scope/):

- Move or duplicate the stickies from the priority triangle exercise into a workspace.
- Place the stickies in the appropriate rows:
  - Who: These are all the departments, resources, process owners, teams, and stakeholders.
  - Won: This is how we measure success; ideally, this is a measurable result or feedback from customers or process performance.
  - Done: When is the project complete? Not a date, but the "last" thing that needs to occur before the project team is disbanded.
- Check and see if you have gaps and fill them with the help of the team.

- Group the stickies by like themes to determine the success criteria—at least three, not more than five.
- Any stickies the team decides don't fit, move into the out-of-scope column.
- Has the group reached a consensus on the success criteria—is it accurate and complete?

As we've said before, this is a key artifact for your project, so keep it on hand for input into the Understand leg and revisiting during the Create leg.

1.4 Resource Strategy

Today's organizations and projects have unique resourcing requirements compared to 30 to 40 years ago. When I started my career in project management, I had dedicated teams assigned to projects where at least 80 percent of their activities were project-focused. You even had dedicated space for the project team to do their work. That is not the case over the last decade.

Matrix organizations have been around for a while and outsourcing of services gained momentum in the 1990s; today, we have even more diverse structures deploying not only matrix organizations but also dynamic teams and specialized vendors and partners. On top of that, we do not have a dedicated collocated workspace for project teams; instead, we have teams that are operating in virtual space in multiple time zones and even on diverse continents.

The strengths of dedicated teams and dedicated project workspaces were:

- Focus for project team members—having one primary focus in terms of not only the work but also one leader, the PM.
- Camaraderie, spontaneous interactions, deeper connection, dynamic real-time problem solving, hallway conversations, face-to-face communication, the "hum" or vibe of a

productive, focused, and passionate team—all the little nuanced things that brought life to teams and projects.

- Visibility—of each other but also within the organization—the rest of the company could see the space the team occupied, how they interacted, visit the space, and ask questions.
- Proximity made it easy to work, visually problem solve, communicate, and celebrate success.

Because of this new environment, the PMGB has tackled these issues by putting a greater emphasis on teams, collaboration, and interactions. Specifically, you'll see this show up in the following:

- Listen leg incorporates a discussion on resourcing strategy—before a project is initiated—which sets up project teams for success.
- Understand leg has extensive material on project team kick-offs to ensure that virtual teams get started on the right foot.
- Create leg also incorporates a project team kick-off as a lot of projects have different resources for planning versus executing.
- Understanding has a step for communication—we want to find the best ways possible to establish communication tools and techniques and then reflect and continuously improve them throughout the project.
- Our use of virtual collaboration best practices also builds project workspaces that energize teams, build personal connections, and make them more resilient.

The Resource Strategy step in the Listen stage of the project is primarily about identifying the groups of people required in terms of employees, vendors, partners, key customers, suppliers, or expert knowledge, skills, or capacity that the organization doesn't have. Don't forget at this stage you are still determining the viability of the project idea, not staffing up the project itself.

We want to keep the resourcing discussion brief and to the point, so key considerations within the strategy will be:

- Who are our stakeholders? Who are the decision makers in these groups?
- What is our approach to addressing the expertise and capacity required?

Let's tackle each of these individually, and then let's specifically discuss resourcing and client projects. Also, don't forget that there is no right or wrong answer to these questions, just information that informs the decision on project viability in step 1.5 Viable Idea, and our Go/No Go at the end of this leg.

Who Are Our Stakeholders and Decision Makers?

The traditional definition of a stakeholder per PMI is:

individuals and organizations who are actively involved in the project, or whose interests may be positively or negatively affected as a result of project execution or successful project completion. (Project Management Institute, PMI®, 1996)[1]

Now how do you select them? What will be their role in the project? Will they have decision-making power? Will their role change over time? All these things need to be considered at this stage of the project. Also note that they don't need to be finalized or set in stone: These roles and responsibilities change at each leg of the PMGB. For the Listen leg of the board, I recommend focusing on decision makers—finding them and pitching your project to get to the next leg of the board.

The customer journey map you completed in 1.2 Contextualize is a key tool to find the decision makers. This gives you insights into the process owners that need to be involved as decision makers. Also, if you have OKR information, look for the highest level in the organization that

---

[1] L.W. Smith. 2000. "Stakeholder Analysis: A Pivotal Practice of Successful Projects," *Paper Presented at Project Management Institute Annual Seminars and Symposium, Houston, TX* (Newtown Square, PA: Project Management Institute).

directly relates to your project and that is another decision maker that needs to be engaged.

Resourcing Approach

The resourcing approach is very straightforward: Remember, we're just looking for potential key knowledge, skill, or capacity gaps. Key questions are:

- Do we have key areas of expertise that are outsourced currently and might be needed by this project? Pay particular attention to the core technologies you identified in your customer journey map—do you have the depth of expertise internally that may be required? This can add complexity and budget considerations to your project as well as affect timelines if you have to go through a procurement cycle, so it's important to identify early in the project.
- Do we have key partners or suppliers that might be impacted or have the expertise to solve this problem? This can help address internal capacity constraints as well as add complexity to the project in terms of negotiating access to these resources that we don't have direct control over.
- Do we currently utilize resourcing models that incorporate contractors versus employees? Again, this can be positive or negative in terms of helping us with internal capacity issues or affecting our timelines and budgets as we procure external resources.

Here's a simple table (Figure 2.9) to capture the resource strategy.

Element	Answer
Insource versus outsource	
Key partners or suppliers	
Employees, contractors, or backfills?	

Figure 2.9 Resources Strategy template

Resourcing and Client Projects

For our client-facing projects, we want to discuss the whos in terms of:

- Who are the decision makers? These are the people who will:
  - o Approve status reports and payments.
  - o Make milestone decisions—assessing organizational readiness to proceed to the next stage, that is, design is complete, we are ready to build, testing is complete, and we are ready to start training.
- Who can complete the deliverables for this project? For many projects, whether it's building a bridge or building a website, there are client resources that will be responsible for delivering content critical to the project's success. I can't count the number of times a website or software project has been delayed due to client content delays!! Have that resource discussion upfront to avoid problems with the project later. Keep in mind that your project is of high priority to you but these resources on the client side may not have this as a priority nor the capacity to respond like you need them to.
- Who has the organizational knowledge we may need to fulfill this project? This is particularly true when our project is trying to leverage client processes and procedures—they can help us navigate these processes and give our project access to resources and visibility for our project. An example of this is the communication department within our client organization— they will have the tools and techniques we can leverage within our project and therefore not have to create our own.

1.5 Viable Idea

In this step, we want to look at all the information we've gathered in this leg and make a decision on whether this idea is a viable project. So, this is our first opportunity to exercise collaborative decision making! To facilitate this decision, the 3P agenda is:

Purpose: Why are we having this meeting? To decide whether this project idea is viable.

Process: What is the process we are going to use to arrive at the payoff?

- Walkthrough of agenda—any expectations or concerns?
- Review of problem statement
- Review of contextual information
- Review of project success definition and priority
- Review of resource strategy
- Decision on project viability:
  - Preliminary vote
  - Round table for each stakeholder to describe why they voted that way
  - Final vote
- Communication from this meeting—who are we telling what and by whom?

Payoff: We have clear support for this project and can proceed to the Go/No Go decision or we stop this idea and not expend any more resources at this time.

So, you should have on hand the following (Table 2.1):

You'll want to assemble your key stakeholders and review all this information to ensure its accuracy and completeness. However, if these steps are ambiguous or substantially incomplete, you will probably require resources to uncover the answers or do a preliminary analysis of what these are. If so, *stop here*, get the resources and/or budget to complete these steps, and then proceed!

Table 2.1 Listen decision content requirements

Element	State
Problem statement	Must have
Contextual information	As much as you can get
Project success definition	Must have
Resource strategy	Must have

So, let's walk through how you would conduct this meeting. The 3P agenda is prescriptive, so no real explanation is required here. However, I've added a couple of things that I've found to be best practices:

- Ensure that you always do a review of the agenda and find out attendees' expectations and concerns with the meeting. This is particularly important during this leg as it may be rare for your stakeholders to be in meetings together—as projects are typically cross-functional and most meetings are vertical or hierarchical.

- I've proposed a collaborative decision technique that is very functional for this type of meeting. It's based on the Delphi decision model (www.thedecisionlab.com/reference-guide/management/the-delphi-method) that leverages the expertise of groups. It's also easy to facilitate and ensure that we get input from each attendee—or key stakeholder (that's why it's so important to have the right people in the room for this meeting). Once you've completed the review of the material in agenda items 2 through 5, have all the attendees vote on whether the project is viable: yes or no. This should be done silently. Then, have each attendee explain the reason why they voted this way. I would set a time limit of a couple of minutes for each person. Also, start with the least senior person in the room and end with the most senior person—in many organizations, this will ensure that their title doesn't sway the voting inadvertently. Once this is completed, vote silently again. There you go—a decision made! If the decision is positive, proceed to Go/No Go and Learn, which we'll cover next. If the decision is no, then you have a choice to table the idea—many organizations might keep it in a backlog of ideas—or shelve it and don't expend any more resources on this idea.

- The last key part of the agenda is the communication from the meeting. It is best practice to conclude a key decision-making meeting (which this is) with a communication plan—who will be told what about the outcome of this meeting? Everyone knows that a meeting with several executive resources will always get the grapevine buzzing—even just developing a robust problem statement will get folks interested in what is happening next. The meeting attendees will be the best folks to decide the method to communicate the result.

If the result of the meeting is that the idea is viable, then the communication is straightforward: it's a go to the next step which is all about determining if this is the right time to proceed with the idea.

If the result of the meeting is not to proceed, the communication is more complicated in that it will depend very much on your organization. It can be as simple as having each meeting attendee communicate to their part of the organization the outcome of the meeting or plugging into whatever communication channel is appropriate and specific to your organization, that is, Slack as a general message, item on a stand-up, or team/corporate huddle. It will be important to communicate not just the decision but also why the project was deemed not viable.

Listen Go/No Go & Learn

This final step in this leg is about two things:

- Examining our viable idea and ensuring now is *the right time* to proceed, given other demands in the organization either operationally or strategically
- Learning how the first leg of our journey went in the spirit of continuous improvement, particularly how to improve our project intake process

These two things are important so that:

- We don't blindly pursue great ideas that don't have the opportunity to be successful due to the demands already underway in the organization.
- We continually improve our project intake processes using retrospectives. I've found that the more organizations improve this intake step, the more sophisticated and effective they are in delivering projects overall.

As in the last step, we are going to use collaborative decision making to facilitate this meeting, but we're going to introduce a new tool, the Possible, Implement, Challenge, Kill (PICK) chart. To facilitate this decision, we've created a 3P agenda template.

Purpose: Why are we having this meeting? To decide on whether this project should proceed to the Understand leg at this time.

Process: What is the process we are going to use to arrive at the payoff?
1. Walkthrough of agenda—any expectations or concerns?
2. Review of project idea (as per viability agenda)
3. Review of project portfolio
4. Go/No Go to proceed with this idea:
   1. Build a PICK chart.
   2. Vote on whether to proceed.
5. Communication from this meeting—who are we telling what?

Payoff: We have clear support for this project and can resource it to develop the plan or we can put this project idea on hold until a more suitable time.

It is important to remember that the decision makers for this meeting may or may not be the same people/roles that attended our previous decision—1.5 Viable Idea. Depending on the size, structure, and roles in your organization, the attendees for this decision need to be able to represent the overall priorities of the organization. For projects already underway, this could be project sponsors; for smaller organizations, this could be either the project customer or PM; for some organizations, this could be a corporate Project Management Office; often this could be a leadership team. To select your attendees, look for three things: Who has the authority, accountability, and responsibility for mandating initiatives to achieve corporate goals? Also, if your organization is using OKRs, this becomes straightforward: It's the folks at the most senior level responsible for the objectives aligned with each of the projects.

The primary tool to be used in the first part of this step is the PICK chart, a great tool to examine different projects relative to each other. It's also a collaborative decision best practice that we'll draw on many times at different steps in the PMGB. For detailed instructions on the PICK chart, refer Chapter 4—Create 3.5 Making Decisions.

If every project idea consistently goes through the Listen steps, then it becomes easier to assess one idea and project relative to others as they will all have at least:

- A problem statement
- Project success criteria and project priority
- Resource strategy

In summary, you would end up with a PICK chart that could look like Figure 2.10.

When you are building the PICK chart, record as much of the discussion as possible because this is invaluable information when another evaluation is done or this may also uncover information to update your project documentation from this leg.

Learn

After each leg, we want to utilize retrospectives to improve our project processes and, in future legs, do a retro on our team culture. As we don't usually have a project team established at this stage, the focus of this retrospective is on how we can improve the steps in this leg. I find that setting up or framing the retrospective is the best first step to ensure that the retrospective adds value. Key questions you'll want to answer are:

- Should/could this be done asynchronously or synchronously? If you've had people participate in this leg from different time zones or that have huge time demands (senior execs are often part of this leg and having them meet can be a project in itself), there may be a case to do this retrospective asynchronously. That also comes with the proviso that they would be familiar with participating in and performing retrospectives and developing corrective action plans regularly.

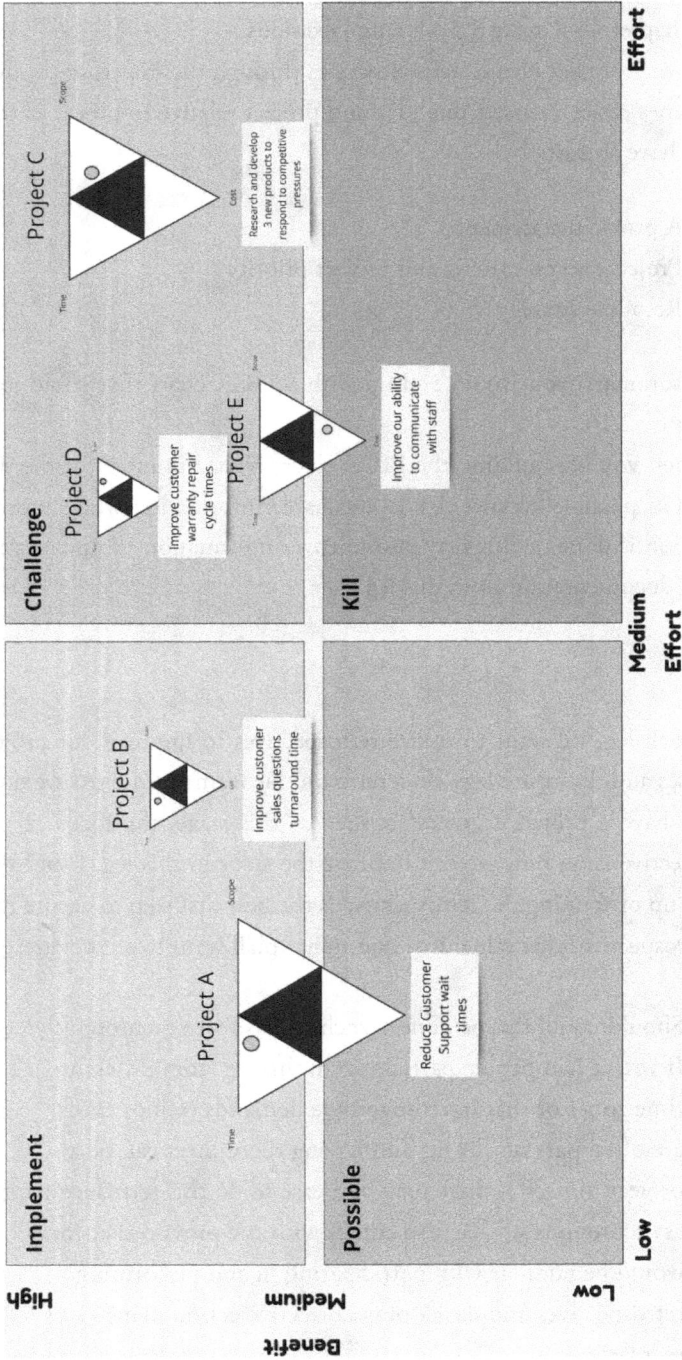

Figure 2.10 PICK chart of multiple projects

Alternatively, if your participants aren't comfortable working asynchronously or can't be counted on to complete the work, then a meeting will work best.

- If your organization is characterized by the dreaded "boiling the ocean" syndrome—tons of concurrent projects, all of them are priority 1, each project puts demands on the same key resources, and none of them seem to conclude, let alone deliver results—then your retrospective is a unique opportunity to try to tame this beast! I've found that incomplete project intake processes create exactly this situation so this is an opportunity to learn, which will have multiple benefits for future projects.

  How deep should/could this retrospective go? If you've struggled to get the required information to complete this step (it's just not available readily), and/or found that different groups are at loggerheads about the project priority, then it usually means that your organization has immature management practices. This is not necessarily a negative—it may just be the stage that an organization is at in its growth. Our job as PMs is not to change senior management but to deliver successful projects—so in this case, emphasis can be placed on having a thorough problem statement and project success criteria that will still set up future projects for success.

- Finally, to whom and how will the learnings from this work be best applied in your organization? If you are an organization that delivers projects to clients, then lessons from this leg will potentially need to feed into the Sales organization to better inform how clients are pitched or onboarded in the future. If you have a Project Management Office, then lessons learned will help inform future projects in the portfolio, so you'll want to structure your retrospective to ensure that it complies with or meets those expectations.

You can summarize your thoughts in Table 2.2.

Table 2.2 Listen retrospective methods

Attribute	Yes	Comments	No
Retrospective standard practice	X	Perform an asynchronous retro	Use our template
Standard project intake processes	X	Either async or sync and frame the retro on how well each element of the process is working. Don't forget to use People, Systems, Methods, Measurement, Materials, Environment, and Management in your framing	Aka boiling the ocean Use our template
Application of the learnings is standardized	X	Ensure that the outputs of your retro are fed back to the PMO or into Sales	Use our template

It's important to remember that the focus of this retrospective is to continuously improve the project intake process in the organization. It's about doing the right project!

Figures 2.11 and 2.12 are a couple of examples of what the PICK chart could look like and the next steps.

In this scenario, the OKRs (1.2 Contextualize) are readily available and clearly identify who is responsible for what. The problem statement was easy to complete but didn't add as much value as the OKRs. The success criteria added value but were difficult to complete due to competing priorities between departments. The resources strategy added some value and wasn't too difficult to complete. Action steps from this retrospective would be to ensure that all new project ideas clearly articulate their

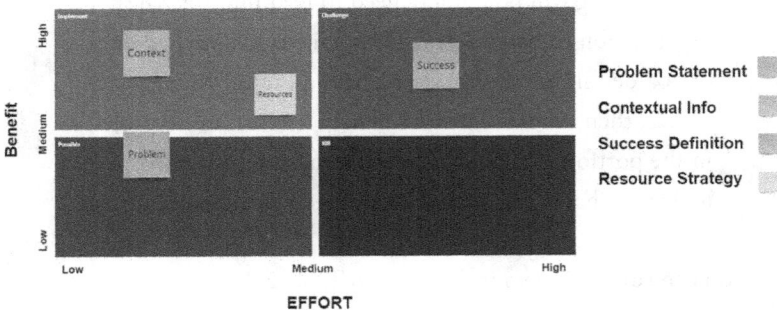

Figure 2.11 PICK for a Listen retrospective—scenario 1

Listen Retrospective

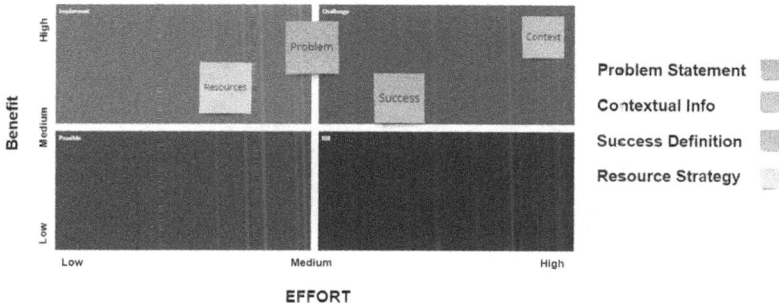

Figure 2.12 PICK for a Listen retrospective—scenario 2

alignment to OKRs. Also, you would want to ensure that the KRs are incorporated into the project success criteria, under the Won section.

In the second scenario, this is what I would expect to find in an organization that is boiling the ocean, has limited or unclear OKRs, and may or may not have customer journey maps. This organization can often make up for these deficiencies by standardizing the project intake process, putting more emphasis on the project problem statement and defining project success thoroughly. This would be the focus of action steps from this retrospective.

In Summary

You made it through the first leg! Congratulations! That means not only have you learned some new tools and techniques but are probably improving the project intake process for your organization and clients!

There are a couple of things that you will have accomplished in this leg:

- A viable project idea that is ready to begin detailed planning.
- A viable project idea that is not ready to begin planning—needs to be tabled and brought back to life at a more appropriate time.
- A project idea that isn't viable and you can stop spending resources on it.
- You have insights into how to improve your project intake process going forward.

CHAPTER 3

Understand—Planning for Success

Transitioning From an Idea to a Project

This is where we transition from an idea—a viable idea—as we completed our due diligence in the Listen leg to the detailed planning for the project. This leg is all about translating our viable idea into deliverables, resource requirements, roles and responsibilities, budgets, timelines, and setting up all the activities that will make the project team successful. This is where the project takes expert knowledge in the organization and translates the 1.3 Success Criteria into specifics that can be created and delivered to add the value required to achieve the objectives of the project. It's important to note that this is often the transition from executive theory to the team determining the practical realities of the project.

For client-based projects, this is where the contract has been negotiated and signed off, and a down payment may have been paid. Given the nature of these procurement activities, there will be a defined budget, a proposed timeline, and some level of the scope defined, so the Understand leg, in this case, will validate these assumptions.

The activities in the Understand leg are built around a culture of freedom and responsibility: clearly understanding each team member's role and having them take ownership of what they are creating. Here's how I define freedom and responsibility:

Project members need to clearly understand their role, have the skills and abilities to perform those duties, and take ownership of what they are delivering to meet customer expectations in terms of time, scope, and quality. Using collaboration in planning and delivering projects ensures that the team can understand, inform, and execute their responsibilities. This is done by providing their input into their project outputs and working together to align them to overall project expectations. They also contribute to the plan and collaborate to ensure the plan is executed to meet expectations.

The art part for any project manager (PM) with these activities will be to select the ones that best allow the team to achieve their role clarity and take ownership by building the plan and yet having the "lightest" touch possible. We want to move away from planning techniques that micromanage resources and are hierarchical or top down. Unlike past practices developed around task management systems that look for the lowest common denominator, we want to find the highest common denominator in our planning efforts and save the details for when we move into the next leg—Create. Our planning needs to be respectful of our team members and allow them to manage their individual task efforts their way. Incorporating collaboration also allows us to harness the expert knowledge and critical thinking of the team.

I've found that project team members have so many different ways of working and managing their day-to-day tasks that are effective for them—they won't be effective for everyone if we try to cram people all into the same methods and software! We'll cover this extensively in the next chapter. In the Understand leg, the emphasis is on ensuring you complete a plan and you use the methods that produce the best results for the team in understanding their roles and responsibilities while still being able to manage expectations and report to customers, sponsors, and key stakeholders of the project.

Moving from a command-and-control environment to a psychologically safe one that balances personal responsibility with corporate responsibility looks like Figures 3.1 and 3.2.

In our Understand Planning, we are focusing on building project plans that highlight the outcomes we are trying to achieve, not the tasks that are required to achieve them. Here are the key differences between outcome-based planning and task-based planning (Figure 3.3).

You can see how the outcomes are much more nuanced and the tasks required to achieve those outcomes can be complex and multifaceted and require the input of the project resources to tease out the project details. This in turn gives them control over their work and harnesses their unique knowledge and abilities.

Command and Control	Psychologically Safe
Characteristics	
Formal Authority	Take Risks/Fail Fast
Chain of Command	Admit mistakes
Discipline	Accountable to outcomes
Processes	Inclusive
Procedures	Adaptive
Policy	Focus on solving problems
Systems	Diverse thinking
Formal Authority	Take Risks/Fail Fast
How it Manifests	
Organizational chart is rigid	Team based
Escalation to resolve issues	Metric based feedback systems
Rigid Job descriptions	Questions are welcomed
Performance plans with formal infrequent feedback	Open to ideas
Inflexible processes, policies, and procedures - lots of rules	Candid feedback
Systems that are inflexible	Collaborative practices

Figure 3.1 Command and control versus psychologically safe

Corporate Responsibility	Personal Responsibility
Characteristics	
Formal job description	Accountability to outcome
Annual performance targets and review	Personal development
Hierarchical hiring	Learn to communicate with diverse audiences and diverse tools
Developmental plans	
How it Manifests	
Developmental plans that don't account for career aspirations	Manage your day-to-day activities
Inflexible roles	Manage your own career path
Job and project assignment by manager	Manage your own development
	Actively solicit feedback from customers
	Admit mistakes
	Identify opportunities for improvement

Figure 3.2 Corporate responsibility versus personal responsibility

Another thing that I've run into countless times with clients over the years is the fact that they don't plan at all! They go from idea to implementation almost immediately and believe that relying on things

Outcome based   ## Task based

> Optimize process performance by improving cycle time

> Implement a task management system

> Standardize the process by implementing and reporting key process milestones and metrics

> Build process dashboard

Versus

> Launch business intelligence software

> Improve customer service by having one place to request service and understand status

> Implement a customer portal

> Track and report customer errors

> Improve the quality of xxx inputs by moving the data entry closer to the customer

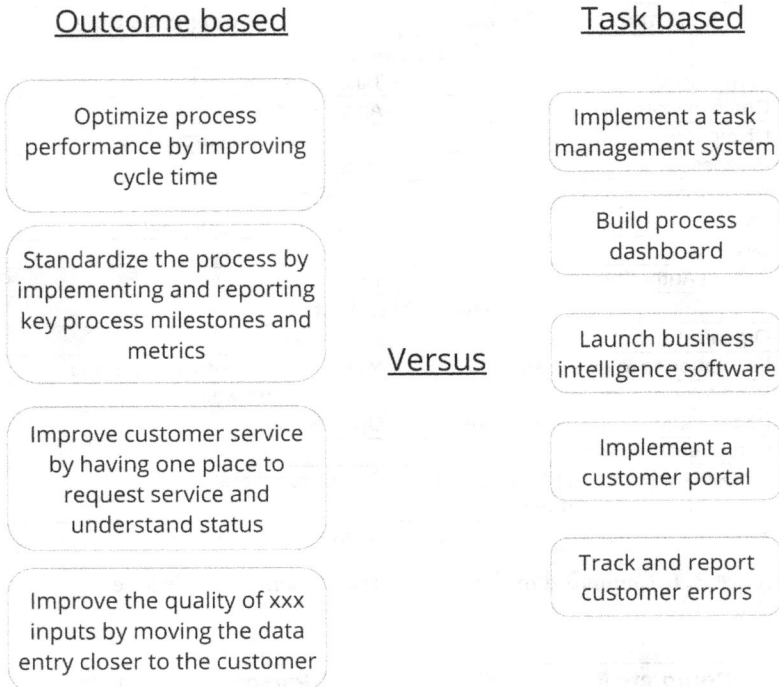

Figure 3.3 Outcome versus task based

like failing fast or iterating means they don't need to plan. As Benjamin Franklin said:

> If you fail to plan you plan to fail.

So, knowing that and wanting to utilize the power of collaboration and the knowledge of the team, I would recommend the following approach to this leg:

- If your organization is notorious for never planning and unwilling to invest the time or resources to do adequate planning, start with the collaborative project charter.
- If you plan projects but are looking to enable more collaboration in your planning practices, start with 2.1 Scope of Work and 2.2 People & Timeline—particularly the planning backward exercise.

- If you already do robust planning, then see which elements of this leg you'd like to explore to mix up or improve planning in your team or build more collaboration.

Just don't forget: Regardless of the type of plans or lack of plans in your organization, project planning starts with a project kickoff and ends with a retrospective!

There are a couple of key activities that are triggered during this leg:

- There is a project team assembled and a Project Manager assigned. It would be ideal if the PM started during the Listen leg, particularly to facilitate the completion of that leg; however, this doesn't always happen.
- With the resources assigned to the project, we can do a project kickoff to create team norms, understand roles and responsibilities, and set up foundational pieces that will benefit us throughout the balance of the project.
- We should develop a plan that is to the level of detail that mitigates the risk of the project meeting its desired outcomes—it needs to be a balance between no plan at all and leaving space for iterating or more Agile methods of delivery. This will involve assessing what level of specificity is required and how the project will acquire and retain the knowledge resources to perform the work. Some of what we did in the Listen leg, particularly around Success Criteria, will inform these decisions.

For the Understand leg (Figure 3.4), we have the steps of:

- Project Team Kickoff: Assembling the team and setting them up for success.
- 2.1 Scope of Work: Breaking down our success criteria and other inputs into concrete deliverables.
- 2.2 People & Timeline: Who is doing what when?
- 2.3 Budget & Equipment: Funding our efforts and sourcing equipment.

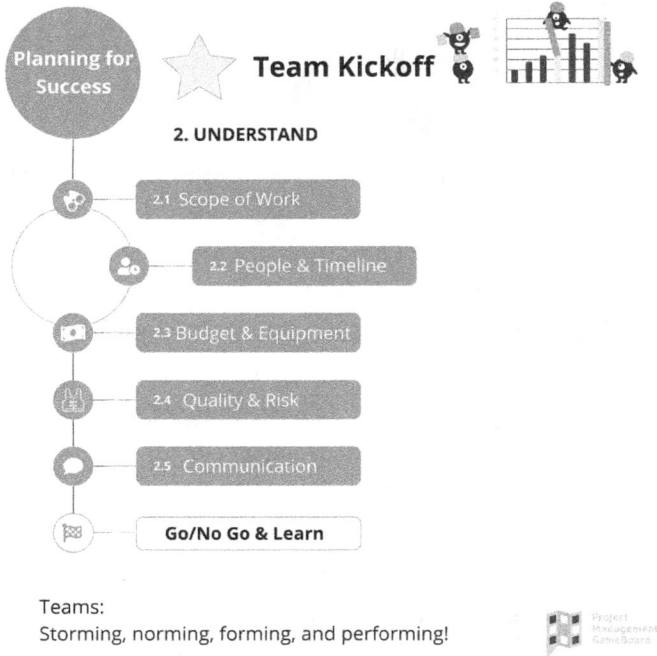

Teams:
Storming, norming, forming, and performing!

Figure 3.4 PMGB understand

- 2.4 Quality & Risk: What are our quality specifications, risk strategy, and tolerance?
- 2.5 Communication: How are we going to communicate with all our stakeholders?
- Go/No Go & Learn: Deciding to go to the next leg— managing expectations—and learning to improve our project planning and check-in with our team.

Project Team Kickoff

This is the critical first step of this leg. As part of this, we need to do several things:

- Decide who will manage the project.
- Assemble the team.
- Kickoff meeting—preparing for and conducting.

Decide Who Will Manage the Project

Selecting a PM varies from project to project and from organization to organization. I've found it can be from one end of the spectrum—what I call the voluntold PM—to a formal role either insourced or outsourced that specializes in project management. For our purposes, we're going to look at this from the perspective of the organization: What are the considerations in managing this project? Questions to address when determining the best fit are as in Table 3.1.

Table 3.1 Understand—project manager fit questions

Question	Type of PM	Consideration
Is this a strategically important project that could put the corporate image at risk internally or externally?	Full-time experienced PM	Insourced if available, outsourced if you have robust PM methods and standards
Is this a strategically important client that is fundamentally challenging our typical delivery model?	Experienced PM	Always insourced but could be part-time
Is there a need to build PM bench strength in the organization?	Full-time PM with an experienced mentor	The mentor could be insourced or outsourced depending on the depth of knowledge in the organization and the availability of PMs

Note: The question wasn't whether there is going to be a PM—if you have truly done your work from the Listen leg and this is a project, then *yes*, it must have a dedicated PM, and then the question has become how you're going to source that PM.

Do We Need a Project Sponsor?

The answer to this question is twofold: What is a project sponsor and then do we need one?

Project sponsors are a relatively new development in project management, and they are not used by all organizations or for all projects. I've found them to be very helpful to projects and PMs to:

- Streamline decision making—dealing with one person instead of a committee.

- Command authority—as a PM often has more influential power than organizational power, they can remove roadblocks, make corporate commitments, and negotiate with peers as well as provide a communication path laterally and upwards in the organization.
- Champion a project within the organization.

Once you understand the following section on customer, then determine not only whether you need a project sponsor but also who the most appropriate sponsor is.

Sponsor Versus Customer

It's interesting to see how the PM's role has changed over the last few decades; some things have changed and some things have stayed the same. Some of the consistent things have been:

- A PM's role is typically done with limited formal or hierarchical authority. This manifests in a couple of ways— the PM is typically managing up when it comes to key stakeholders. PMs need to know how to wield influence more than authoritative control to be effective. They also often don't have direct authority over the people on the project team; they typically don't select the resources assigned to the team and have limited direct authority over them—project resources usually report to an operating manager.
- A project team rarely has dedicated resources assigned to the project. Either the resources are working on multiple projects (think of development teams) or sharing their project duties with their operational duties.

Some newer developments in projects have been:

- Development of the role of a project sponsor. This has occurred over the last 20 years and is meant to address some of the organizational power imbalances mentioned earlier as this role is typically fulfilled by a senior manager. I've found these roles can be very effective—much more effective than having the PM report to a committee, as long they fulfill their responsibilities of:

  o Providing project funding.
  o Ensuring resources are appropriate and available for the project.
  o Approving the project documents.
  o Monitoring the status of the project and ensuring ongoing alignment of the project with the strategic goals and vision of the organization.
  o "Open doors" to resources outside the specific scope of the project that may be required.
  o Understanding they may be responsible for following up on, measuring, and reporting on the project's return on investment (ROI) once it has been completed in three to six months.

- The critical role of the subject matter expert (SME). This term came from the world of building business requirements in IT projects—they were the folks who had frontline or hands-on experience with business processes and transactions and could provide insights into how technology needed to be developed. It is now a critical role in every project as there is so much specialized knowledge in any project; whether it be specific product knowledge on a construction project or business knowledge.

- One thing to remember about sponsors is that they aren't the customers of the project! The customer is the senior manager who receives the outputs or outcomes of the project; the sponsor is the resource that ensures that the project is done correctly and removes barriers to the project's success. One additional differentiator between the sponsor and the customer is that the customer will be responsible for measuring and achieving the ROI for the project after it's delivered. This is usually at least three-plus months down the road after the project team has been disbanded and the project has been operationalized.

Now, after all this discussion, Table 3.2 may help you decide how to assemble the management structure for the project.

Table 3.2 Project organization structure questions

Question	Consideration	Recommended management structure
Is this a strategically important project that could put the corporate image at risk internally or externally?	These are typically customer or employee-facing projects and, while the customer is often sales/customer service or finance/HR, a C-suite sponsor ensures the project has the executive profile and departmental independence	Full-time experienced PM C-suite sponsor Customer most closely aligned with the problem to be resolved
Is this a strategically important new product or service that is fundamentally changing our delivery model?	Again, the customer would be the product development or marketing group. A C-suite sponsor ensures the project has the executive profile and departmental independence. Also, these types of projects across departments and their authority level and relationship with peers will be critical to the success of the project	Full-time experienced PM C-suite sponsor Customers from the department best aligned (most skin in the game) for the new product rollout
Is there a need to build PM bench strength in the organization?	Having distinct sponsor and customer roles can improve project knowledge and cross-functional organizational knowledge or bench strength	Experienced PM, experienced sponsor, and customer
Does the customer of the project have limited project management/sponsorship experience?	Having an experienced sponsor can help the PM and customer during the project	Experienced PM, experienced sponsor, and customer

Assemble the Team

Given the work we've done in Listen, this should be a relatively easy exercise! We know from 1.2 Contextualize through either the OKRs or customer journey map who our key stakeholders are—so these are our departments, teams, and knowledge areas to gather our resources from. Approaching these executives is the place to start identifying the resources that are needed on the team to build the plan.

The only addition to this conversation will be a discussion with these same executives about backfills—the strategy of filling an operational role with a new resource for the duration of this leg of the project. I recommend that this be discussed as part of the resourcing strategy with the department, which will allow the project planning to get underway with the most knowledgeable resources. This will ensure that the project plan has the most knowledgeable people developing the plan as well as identifying backfill requirements—timing and budget before commencing the next leg.

Project Kickoff Meeting

We have a unique ability to create our own culture in project teams. Key to getting our project team off on the right foot is the project kickoff meeting. In this meeting, we want to begin the process of building a great team and a great project culture. So, let's review the elements of a great kickoff meeting, and how you prepare for it and conduct it!

A good project kickoff meeting has a few key elements:

- All the information from the Listen leg needs to be shared with the team.
- Any lessons learned from previous phases of a project or similar projects need to be shared and built upon to have the team decide how they will mitigate or incorporate them into this project.
- Set up space and time for the team to develop their team norms. These can be based on existing corporate culture or corporate values or developed by the team itself during a brainstorming exercise.
- Develop the roles and responsibilities of each team member. There is a generic roles and responsibilities template that is a good starting point. The template is available at www .pmgameboard.com/product/project-roles-and-responsibilities- template/. Also, communicate the role of the PM and the project sponsor.

- Determine the team communication strategy. A good starting point is to have each project team member understand that they are responsible for being the eyes and ears of the project in their "home" team or department and that they are responsible for communicating from the project team to their "home" team or department, particularly when it comes to decisions, key meetings, and milestones. For larger projects, particularly those that have direct customer impact, it is often beneficial to have a communications resource as part of the project team to provide advice on how to leverage existing communication channels.

To make your meeting successful, here's a recommended agenda that we'll review in detail, so you're ready to go.

Purpose: Why are we having this meeting? To build relationships and cocreate our team norms.

Process: What is the process we are going to use to arrive at the payoff?

1. Expectations and concerns
2. Review of Listen outputs
3. Roles and responsibilities—process owner or SME
4. Review the next steps in Understand:
    a. 2.1 Scope of Work
    b. 2.2 People & Timeline
    c. 2.3 Budget & Equipment
    d. 2.4 Quality & Risk
5. Lessons learned—existing or new
6. Team norms

Payoff: We understand our role in the project and have a set of team norms that will make us successful!

For the Listen outputs part of the agenda, take the elements from your 1.4 Viable Idea meeting and content from the Go/No Go meeting and prep them to brief your project team.

For roles and responsibilities, start with the template and update based on the teams' feedback.

Next on the agenda are the three main elements of the Understand leg that the project team members will be involved in. You'll want to brief them on these steps, what they are, and their role in building these parts of our plan. Here's a summary of the key activities:

- 2.1 Scope of Work: SMEs and decision makers will brainstorm deliverables based on the inputs from the Listen leg and their knowledge and skills.
- 2.2 People & Timeline: The team will collaborate to develop a detailed resource plan, RACI, and timeline to build the deliverables identified in the scope.
- 2.3 Budget & Equipment: The team will build a budget based on pessimistic, likely, and optimistic estimates and any equipment requirements for the project.
- 2.4 Quality & Risk: The team will outline the roles, responsibilities, and potential measures of quality and build risk profiles and mitigation plans.

The next part of our meeting will be lessons learned: This refers to what we can learn or have learned from previous projects that may apply to this project. That can be done in a couple of ways. Ideally, we have information from previous projects that we can learn from or perhaps a previous phase of this same project. The important part is not to be too literal with these previous lessons—try and have as broad a context as possible. For example, if this is an IT-focused project—a key deliverable is a new system or a major change to a key corporate system—examine another IT-focused project regardless of the system or department involved and see what you can learn. This learning can be in the form of retrospectives that they've done in the project—from any phase of the project—or you could invite key members from the previous project to share what they learned with your team directly.

Finally, for our project kickoff, we want to build team norms: How is this project team going to behave, interact, and especially measure culture and performance? If you have a set of corporate values, that's a great starting point. Use these as an overview and have the team brainstorm how they are going to demonstrate these in the project. If these don't exist, then I recommend having the team build its own set of norms.

When developing these, just make sure that they are clearly understood by everyone—it can help to have the team describe the behaviors that demonstrate these norms and particularly those that don't.

There is an entire section of the Miroverse dedicated to team building. Check out this section and look for templates that fit your style and culture around developing norms and getting to know each other better. A good template will have not just hard skills but soft skills and some personal information as well!

Collaborative Project Charter

As we mentioned earlier, if your organization typically doesn't plan at all, the collaborative project charter can be a simple place to start—both collaborating and planning! It's a template developed from the material from the Project Management Institute's Educational Foundation and is available through a Creative Commons license.

Here's what the template looks like (Figure 3.5):

A PDF copy of this template is available at www.pmgameboard.com/product/one-page-project-charter-template/.

As we do with so many of these activities, let's start with our meeting agenda.

Purpose: Why are we having this meeting? To cocreate a project charter.
Process: What is the process we will use to get to the payoff?
1. Icebreaker.
2. Introductions: Why are you here?
3. Workshop each element of the charter.
4. Review the charter overall to check for conflicts, gaps, and further input required.
Payoff: To create a project charter that will guide our work and meet our customers' expectations.

Then let's take each element of the charter and review some highlights or considerations (Table 3.3).

As you're building the charter, you will also have the added benefit of having the team provide input and feedback immediately! Once the

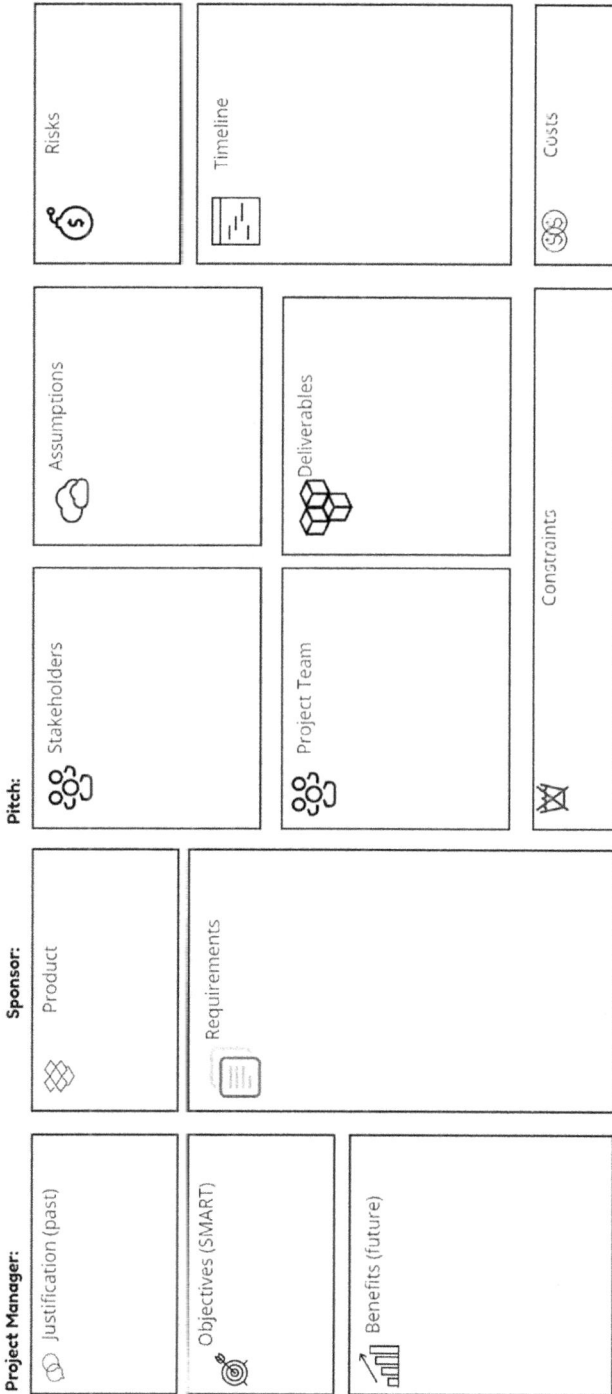

Project Manager: **Sponsor:**   **Pitch:**

Justification (past)

Objectives (SMART)

Benefits (future)

Product

Requirements

Stakeholders

Project Team

Assumptions

Deliverables

Constraints

Risks

Timeline

Costs

Figure 3.5 Collaborative project charter

Table 3.3 Collaborative project charter elements

Element	Considerations
Justification	This is the background to the project—this could be elements from the Listen leg. How did you get to this point? This could be prepared in advance
Objectives	What are we trying to achieve with this project—if you can—make sure they are SMART (specific, measurable, achievable, relevant, and time-bound)?
Benefits	What will be realized when this project is complete?
Product	Is there anything that is going to be produced as a result of the project? Also note this could be the introduction of a new service or process as opposed to a physical product
Requirements	What are the requirements to build this product or service?
Stakeholders	All the interested parties
Project team	All those involved in the project
Assumptions	Note any assumptions the team makes in preparing the charter
Deliverables	There may be some overlap here with requirements but it's important to highlight here key stages or outputs of the project along the way
Risks	What could occur to derail this project?
Timeline	What are the key time increments of the project? Are there key decisions to be made at distinct periods of time?
Constraints	What could constrain this project—what limitations could we encounter?
Costs	What is our budget or anticipated costs to complete this project?

charter is complete, I would recommend reviewing it with your project sponsor and project customer to get their feedback. If that's all your organization is ready for at this time, then get this charter done, and now skip to Go/No Go & Learn!

2.1 Scope of Work

Critical to scoping the project is to involve the right people in translating the high-level requirements determined in the Listen leg into meaningful and actionable deliverables by resources that understand them. That means we'll be utilizing some collaboration practices to leverage the knowledge of these key resources. The collaborative workshops also have the benefit of moving quickly—project planning can take hours and days, not weeks and months. Also, by having the people responsible for the deliverables build the plan, we increase ownership and accountability for those deliverables.

The workshops that I recommend to develop a robust yet flexible/adaptive project plan are:

1. Completing or updating the customer journey map
2. Translating success criteria into deliverables
3. Building a plan backwards
4. Preparing PLO estimates and a critical path
5. Preparing the budget and equipment requirements based on the foregoing

Also, don't forget that steps 2.1 Scope of Work, 2.2 People & Timeline, and 2.3 Budge & Equipment are circular. After you complete each one, circle back and see if there are any implications for the previous work completed.

Customer Journey maps

We talked about customer journey maps in Chapter 2—Listen; however, it isn't unusual for a project team to revisit the high-level customer journey map and break it down into more detail to develop the scope of the project. The same format applies, but the bulk of the work would be in identifying more details around the process/actions row, gathering or updating KPI baseline information, and/or gathering or updating customer sentiment data. This information will provide further detail on the success criteria and build the project deliverables into specifics.

Translating Success Criteria Into Project Deliverables

For *each* success criteria:

- Brainstorm deliverables (goods to be delivered or services performed) that will support the achievement of this success.
- Affinity chart or group the ideas by commonality.
- Apply the PICK chart to prioritize the deliverables.
- Repeat for each success criterion.

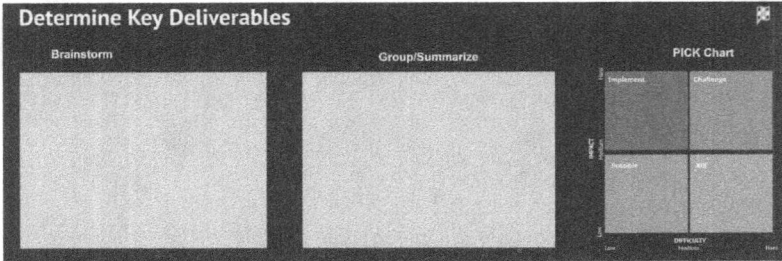

Figure 3.6 Deliverables brainstorm

The template for this work is shown in Figure 3.6. There is a PDF version of this template available at www.pmgameboard.com/shop/scope-feasibility-template/ and a Miroverse version at www.miro.com/miroverse/project-scope/.

You'll end up with a board that looks like the one shown in Figure 3.7 (with a section for each success criterion).

Note that this will typically need to be validated with your project sponsor and customer.

If you want to integrate some of this into your Agile practices, think of Figure 3.8.

The themes would be the input we generated from 1.2 Contextualize in the Listen leg.

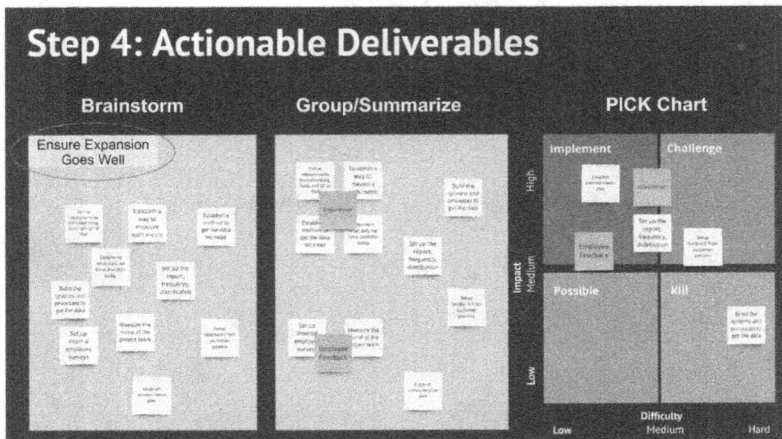

Figure 3.7 Actionable deliverables example

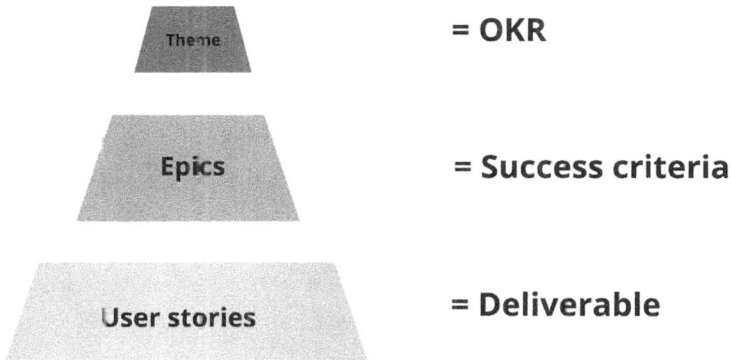

Figure 3.8 Agile versus PMGB

For projects that are client focused (projects within your process), don't skip this step! However, you will only need to brainstorm deliverables for any success criteria that don't align with your standard delivery model. For example, if the client has five success criteria and four of them align with your standard delivery model, just work on that one success criterion and don't forget to validate with the client when you're done.

Also, don't forget that you may uncover out-of-scope items from this exercise—they are the ones in the "kill" quadrant of the PICK chart. Be sure and document those for future reference.

2.2 People & Timeline

When it comes to people and timeline, don't forget the iterative circle between 2.1 Scope of Work, 2.2 People & Timeline, and 2.3 Budget & Equipment. We'll spend time on key collaborative planning techniques for the timeline, as well as talk about the more detailed resource plan to match scope with resources, but we also want to spend some time talking about procurement activities. This is an area often not given the attention it deserves and, when done poorly, can dramatically affect our project performance as well as our team performance, so we'll spend time on that as well.

Now that we know our scope of work (see Figure 3.9), we can build the timeline and details of the resource plan for our project. We do that again with a collaborative workshop that utilizes planning backwards—seeing

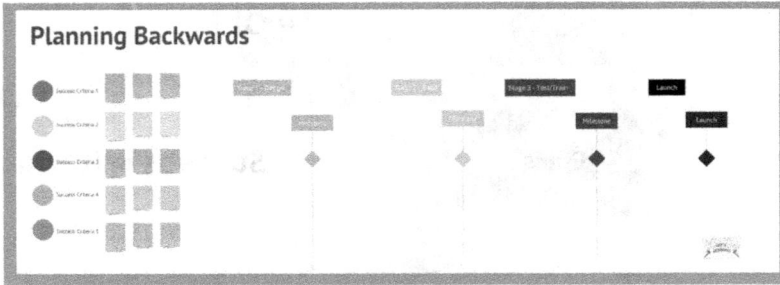

Figure 3.9 Planning backwards template

the beginning from the end. Using this method will allow us to see the interrelationship between deliverables at different stages/phases of the project—check for gaps and do the critical thinking about deliverables between the success criteria.

Timeline

Building a Plan Backwards

Our high-level deliverables need to be assessed for alignment, completeness, and interdependencies. This method of visual critical thinking will ensure our plan is robust:

- Identify a color for each of your success criteria: Place the criteria in the top left corner of the template.
- Translate each of your deliverables from your PICK chart into the colors to match the success criteria. (See the example in Figure 3.9.)
- Put the stickies into a sequence moving backwards from launch to today.
- Stand back and have the project team see if there are gaps or key deliverables that have been missed and complete those.
- Repeat until you've gone through all the success criteria.

The template to complete this exercise is in Figure 3.9. Also this template is available at www.pmgameboard.com and a Miroverse version at www.miro.com/miroverse/project-timeline-builder/.

Here are some tips and tricks when preparing the backwards plan:

- We have specifically used the terms Design, Build, Test/ Train, and Launch: These could apply to a lot of projects. If you don't think these terms apply to your project, feel free to change them; however, also ask why they don't apply to your project and what replaces them. Here are some other industry-specific models in Figures 3.10 and 3.11. These templates are also available at www.pmgameboard.com/shop/ planning-backward-stages-template/.
- This is the step that will move the planning from the senior management team to the project team: Having the project team create this part of the plan will improve accountability and ownership!
- Doing this collaboratively may seem like a lot of work, but don't forget about the hidden benefits of doing the plan this way! The team will more thoroughly understand what is expected of them and, even better, they will understand what is expected of each other—a critical component of cross-functional teams.

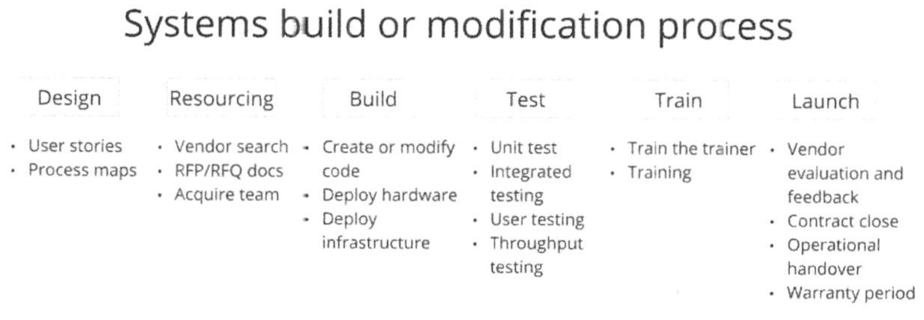

Systems build or modification process

Design	Resourcing	Build	Test	Train	Launch
· User stories · Process maps	· Vendor search · RFP/RFQ docs · Acquire team	· Create or modify code · Deploy hardware · Deploy infrastructure	· Unit test · Integrated testing · User testing · Throughput testing	· Train the trainer · Training	· Vendor evaluation and feedback · Contract close · Operational handover · Warranty period

Figure 3.10 System build model

Product development process

Research	Design	Resourcing	Build	Test	Launch
· Market · Technology · Competition	· Determine minimum viable product · Specifications	· Vendor search · Bid/tender docs · Acquire team	· Create product	· Component test · Integrated testing · Functional test · Target user testing	· Vendor evaluation & feedback · Contract close · Production evaluation

Figure 3.11 Product development model

- Don't get lost in the minutia of what's to be done! Remember that we want to focus on key outputs and handoffs to either the customer or other project team members, not the details of what each person is doing.

Preparing PLO Estimates and a Critical Path

Now that you have all your deliverables, you can start to build the elapsed time required to complete the deliverables. This will inform your timeline, resource plan, and risks. The key technique I use to ensure that timelines are achievable is a collaborative planning workshop with PLO (pessimistic, likely, and optimistic) estimates.

I've been using PLOs for over 20 years to manage project budgets and sponsor expectations. Over all the years, or decades, that I've been using PLO estimates, I've found it leads to project plans and timelines that are never wrong! Honestly, that may be hard to believe but in decades of experience having the team do PLO estimates has led to project timelines—barring an extraordinary event—that are *always* right. Now, sometimes, I've bumped up against the pessimistic estimate but…it truly does work!

This is all about estimating—PLO estimates. These are defined as how long it will take to complete the deliverable under the following conditions:

- Pessimistic: if absolutely everything goes wrong—this includes the worst case within the project and also by external factors, particularly think about resource availability when you have project team members that aren't dedicated to the project.
- Likely: if things are "normal"—if you've done this type of deliverable before, this is a great benchmark.
- Optimistic: if things were absolutely ideal—we had the best people, with no other commitments, and no surprises.

For PLO estimates:

- From your planning backwards template, duplicate or copy your deliverables and convert them to long stickies.
- For each one, complete the PLO estimates of the time required to complete them in the boxes provided.

After completing all the aforementioned steps, you'll have a timeline that looks something like Figure 3.12.

Here are some tips and tricks when building this:

- Don't have any durations longer than two weeks; if you do, break them down into multiple deliverables.
- Make sure the team is clear on whether you are using calendar days or business days to do the estimating.
- Ensure the team is consistently using duration—as opposed to effort. This is more appropriate as we are trying to understand the dependencies between people and their deliverables. If you put these in terms of effort, you will most likely end up in a bun fight about why someone came up with that estimate or questioning one person's productivity. That is a separate discussion and not appropriate during this exercise. We want people to come up with their own estimates and be responsible for them.
- Ranges supply additional information (more on that later):
  o Uncertainty.
  o Possible risks.
  o Different opinions and rationales.
  o Cross-checks.

Once this is complete, look for the ones with the longest pessimistic estimate within each milestone and circle them. The sum of the pessimistic estimates + 30 percent is your project time estimate and also your critical path. On your Miro board, it would look like Figure 3.13.

Bringing the Plan Altogether

To finalize the timeline, you'll need to do a "corporate" view of the plan; I've found that presenting to senior management, your sponsor, and the customer is best done with a simplified view of the plan. Having done the PLOs, you'll now have a timeline that can be translated into Figure 3.14.

Don't forget that this timeline won't have calendar dates on it yet; that will come in the next leg of the project—Create (Implementation). We're focused on the elapsed time for the project at this stage, and translating

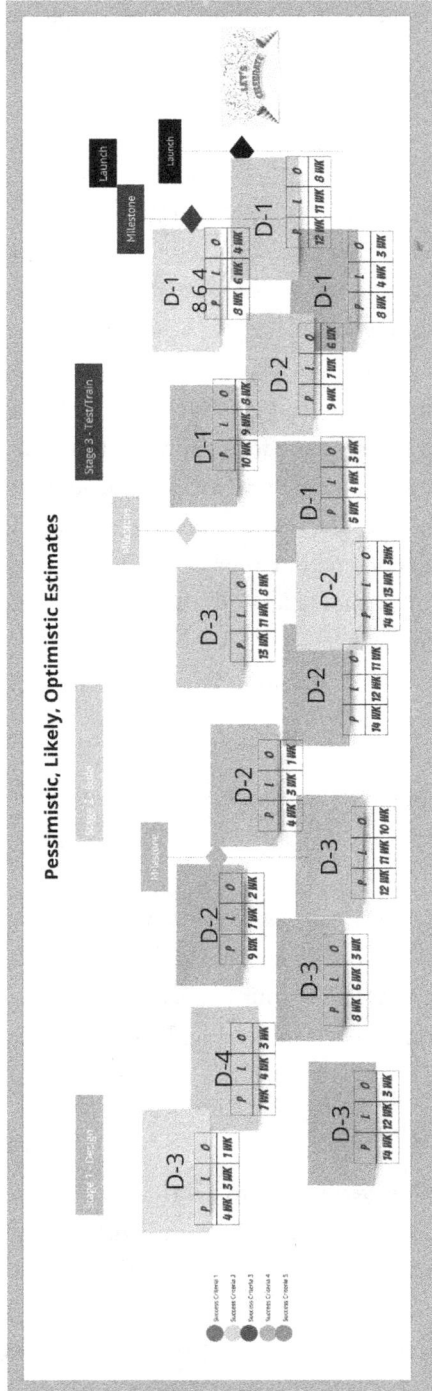

Figure 3.12 Plan backwards with PLOs

Critical path

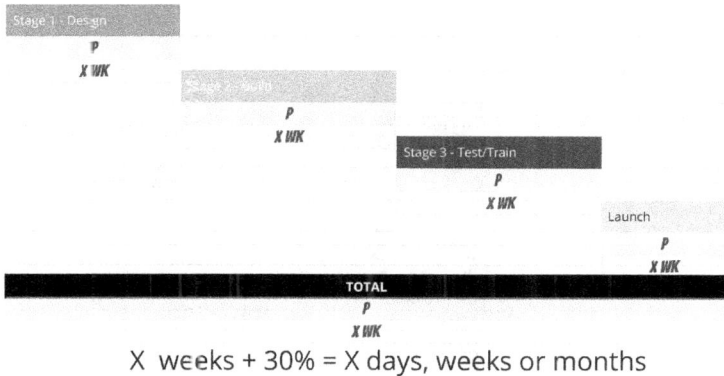

X weeks + 30% = X days, weeks or months

Figure 3.13 Critical path

the plan into dates is part of the next leg and our translation into your task management system of choice.

Resource Plan

To develop the resource plan, we can reuse some of what we've already built in the timeline exercises earlier. Then, we can utilize a new RACI tool that I discovered from Kenbra Deere when she worked at H&R Block. It focuses on relationships and is much easier to use than traditional RACI charts.

For our resource plan, it's as simple as overlaying the resources to your backwards plan. You'll just need to add roles overtop of the deliverables per the example in Figure 3.15.

Here, each deliverable has a dot for each resource or multiple resources when people are cocreating a deliverable. Once you've mapped that out, you can summarize the results into the resource plan template (Figure 3.16).

To determine the decision makers, look for the customer of those deliverables or the process owner. These are the folks that will "accept" that deliverable. Also, I've provided you with space to designate either teams of people to be responsible for those success criteria and their associated deliverables or individual resources.

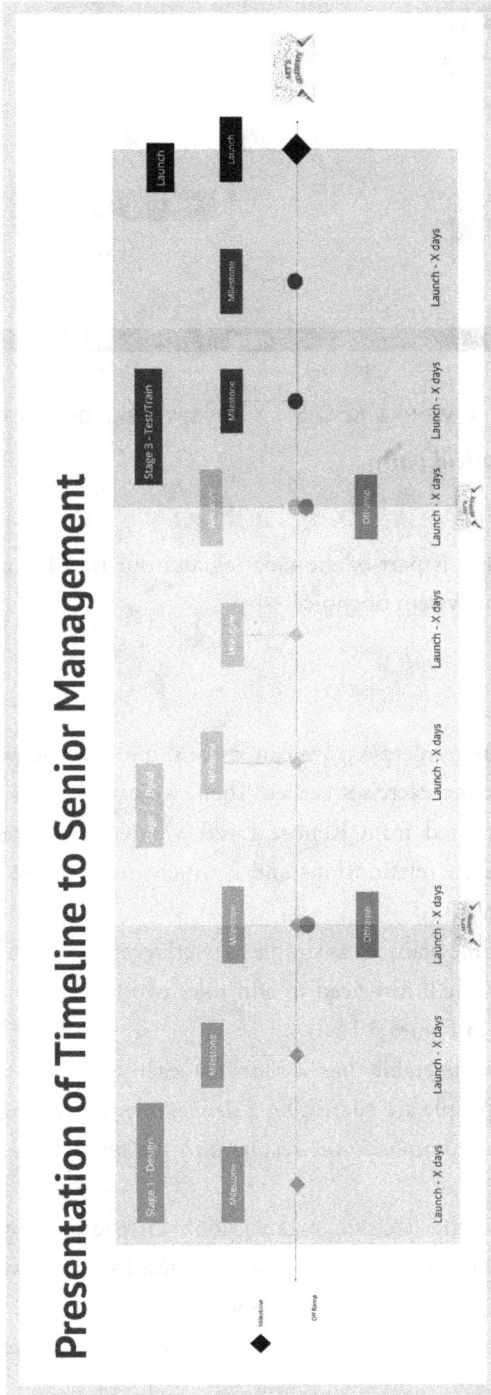

Figure 3.14 Timeline presentation

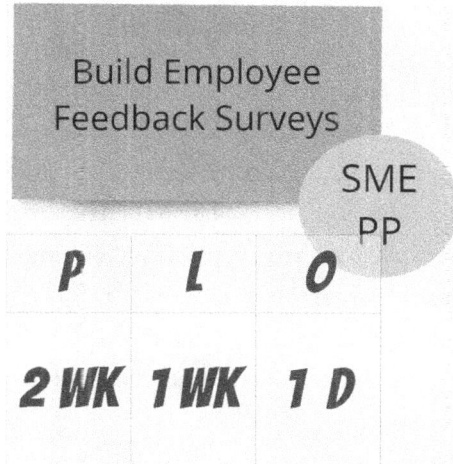

Figure 3.15 Deliverables assignment example

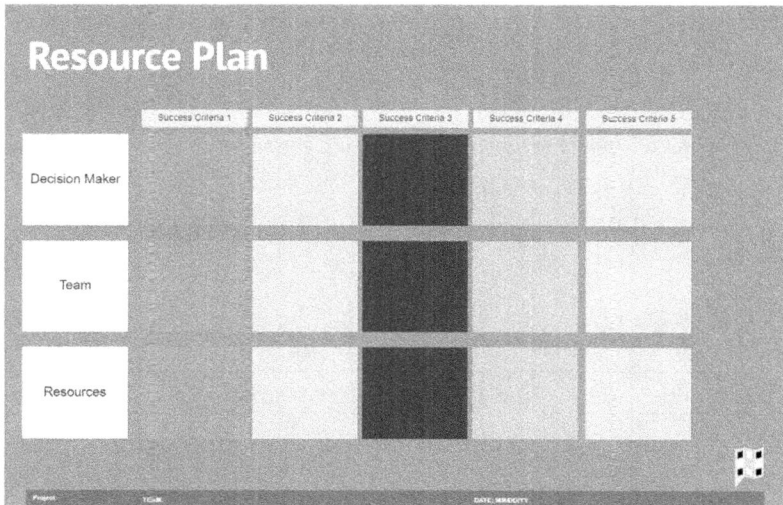

Figure 3.16 Resource plan

Also, when building your resource plan, an important consideration is to look for opportunities to develop organizational knowledge, acquire new skills, and mentor people within the project. With these opportunities, you may bring onboard new resources when we are implementing the plan in the next leg. So, we'll go through another kickoff to ensure we get these folks started on the right foot as well.

Finally, when building the resource plan, don't forget to check back on step 1.4 Resource Strategy to see if we've accounted for any external resources or backfills that are anticipated for the project. Because you've now built your timeline and better understand the scope to be delivered, you are in a better position to assess the implications of core technologies and resource constraints, so don't hesitate to update the resource strategy as required as well as ensure that your plan allows the time needed to acquire and onboard resources needed externally.

To finalize our resource plan, let's build a RACI chart. I have used RACI charts for years—you know the ones that look like alphabet soup! See Table 3.4.

I have never found a team that understands these after they are created or uses them during the delivery of a project—keeping them up to date and meaningful is a nightmare. I have found a RACI template that works because it focuses on relationships (www.miro.com/miroverse/stakeholder-raci-map/).

The beauty of this map is it allows you to visualize the relationships between stakeholders (Figure 3.17). Also, I can't count how many times I've had teams apply ARCI instead of RACI—which isn't a problem, except when the whole team doesn't apply it consistently.

Table 3.4 RACI example

Deliverable	Pete	Sue	Ahmed	Rose	Michaela	Jose	Phil
Deliverable 1	R	A	A	A	C	I	I
Deliverable 2	A	A	A	R	C	C	C
Deliverable 3	R	A	I	I	A	A	I
Deliverable 4	C	C	C	R	A	A	A
Deliverable 5	A	A	A	R	C	C	C
Deliverable 6	I	C	C	I	I	A	R
Deliverable 7	I	I	C	A	A	R	A
Deliverable 8	I	R	I	A	I	A	A
Deliverable 9	I	C	R	A	A	I	C
Deliverable 10	C	I	I	C	R	A	A

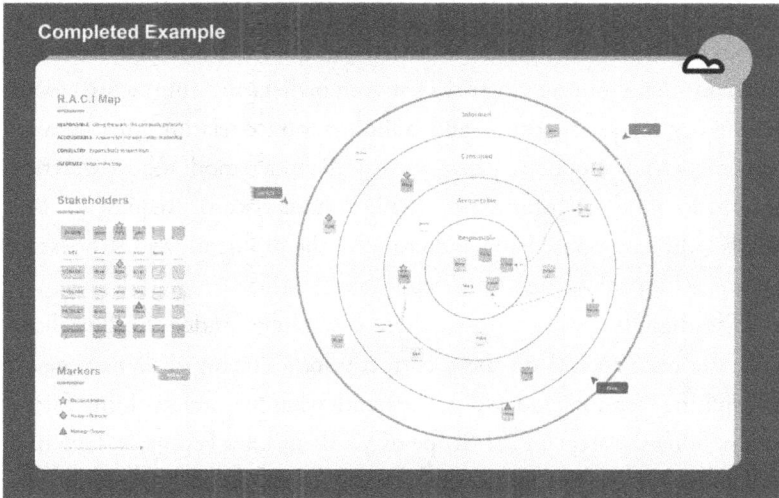

Figure 3.17 RACI

To complete your RACI, follow the instructions on the template and then here are a couple of additional tips and tricks:

- You can use key deliverables as the categories (sticky color) to classify or group the stakeholders.
- Another option is to use categories of stakeholders—insourced versus outsourced and employees versus consultants versus contractors versus suppliers. For projects with many external resources and procurement considerations, this can work well.
- You may want two views for the same project: one by deliverable and another by type of resource.
- Remember that you need to continually update this chart and when you add new resources, make sure you are also onboarding them with the same material you used in your project kickoff meeting at the start of this leg.

Procurement

As I mentioned earlier, this is an area that is critical to project success but often done poorly. I think this is increasing or deteriorating depending on your point of view! By the 1980s and 1990s, procurement practices had moved from contracts, purchase orders, and change orders to more robust conversations about moving risks between owners and contractors, establishing vendor report cards, and building robust relationships between customers and suppliers. There were well-understood robust practices around Request for Information (RFI; a market scan), Request for Proposals (RFP; a proposed approach to solve the problem), and Request for Quote (RFQ; committed time, scope, and cost).

The digital age has thrown these disciplines under the bus; however, the need to still do these correctly hasn't changed! When we are researching vendors, do we understand what we are looking for? If you've done the steps in 2.1 Scope of Work and 2.2 People & Timeline, you should. Then I've found the best way to approach researching vendors is to look for experts in that arena who can refer you to resources or providers. Don't forget to tap into your project team and organizational network; they may have existing relationships that can help facilitate an introduction.

The next artful step I've found is to evaluate proposals; traditionally, this was often done with an extensive list of detailed requirements in a Word doc or equivalent that was thrown over the wall to possible vendors to respond to under very strict timelines and with limited interactions with the direct businesspeople. Over the last decade, I've found this truly doesn't work—in my more cynical moments, I've put it down to that vendor's lie. However, the reality is that it's impossible to document requirements adequately—our organizations and our technology environments are too complex and changing too rapidly!

I've found that a more effective and time-sensitive way to perform this evaluation is to come up with criteria for what will make this relationship successful, weigh their importance, and then score each vendor to determine whether they meet these criteria or not. You'll have a matrix that looks something like Figure 3.18.

This can then be translated into numerical values like in Figure 3.19.

This all begs the question of how you evaluate each of the criteria; that depends on what you're seeking. If it's a software package, get demos and references; if it's procuring contract resources as backfills or PMs, get to know the resources they propose and interview them. In all cases, get references and don't just rely on the references the vendor proposes; make

Weighted Scoring Matrix	Weight	Alternative 1 Score	Alternative 2	Alternative 3
Criterion 1	High	Meet	Not met	Meet
Criterion 2	High	Exceed	Meet	Exceed
Criterion 3	Medium	Not met	Exceed	Meet
Criterion 4	Medium	Exceed	Meet	Not met
Criterion 5	High	Meet	Not met	Meet

Figure 3.18 Procurement weighted scoring v1

Weighted Scoring Matrix	Weight	Alternative 1 Score	Alternative 2	Alternative 3
Criterion 1	10	1	0	1
Criterion 2	10	2	1	2
Criterion 3	5	0	2	1
Criterion 4	5	2	1	0
Criterion 5	10	1	0	1
		50	25	45

Figure 3.19 Procurement weighted scoring v2

sure that the reference looks like your situation and is not just a banner account that gets special treatment. Also, don't hesitate to ask about corporate culture: What are their values? What types of values do they promote? Are they aligned with those of your organization?

It is important to actively engage in conversations with suppliers and vendors. It will give you the opportunity to better utilize their expertise, potentially uncover risks you weren't aware of, and ensure that you are getting a fair price.

Finally, set up your vendor evaluation once the contract is completed, with regular feedback and monitoring of performance. If you can ensure that your procurement processes support these steps, you'll go a long way to improving the potential success of your project and your team!

2.3 Budget & Equipment

The third step of our iterative planning—remember we mentioned earlier—is our budget and equipment. Again, we'll want to build on what we've already developed in 2.1 Scope of Work and 2.2 People & Timeline; we'll complete the budget by using PLOs, but this is focused on effort.

Once more, we've built a template to help you calculate this, thanks to my colleague and Excel guru, Jon White. See Figure 3.20.

To complete this template, you'll populate the tasks by utilizing the information obtained in your PLO workshop. Then add in the resources that are working on each deliverable as a proportion of their time. when you have more than one person on the deliverable, the percentages will add up to more than 100. Finally, add a rate for each resource. This is a budget so no need to get into each person's salary or hourly rate; in fact, if your organization doesn't typically budget for internal resource time, then I recommend using a rate of $100 per hour, which is representative of a fully loaded cost for an internal white-collar job.

Once completed, the spreadsheet will spit out your weighted project cost by each task; that's your opportunity to do a gut check: Does this cost make sense? Do the costs relative to each other make sense? For example, are there tasks that you shouldn't be expending that much money on? Then go back to your PLO estimate or the number of people assigned and adjust accordingly.

Another way to use the PLO is to establish the range of budget required. I find this particularly helpful when a project is focused on time and scope; the organization will use money to deliver to the required schedule. In this case, providing the sponsor and customer with the project ranges gives you a range to work within as opposed to one specific number.

Finally, I recommend rounding the task total to the largest 100s of dollars; this is a budget number, and it shouldn't leave people with a different perception of its accuracy by putting it to the penny or even dollars.

Once you've completed the budget amount for resources, don't forget to add in equipment budget items; this can be anything from scaffolding required during construction to computer equipment required for additional onsite resources.

Agile Versus PMGB

Just before we wrap up these three steps in this leg, let's have a brief discussion about project planning versus Agile. The PMGB is not intended to replace Agile; it is intended to complement whatever methods your

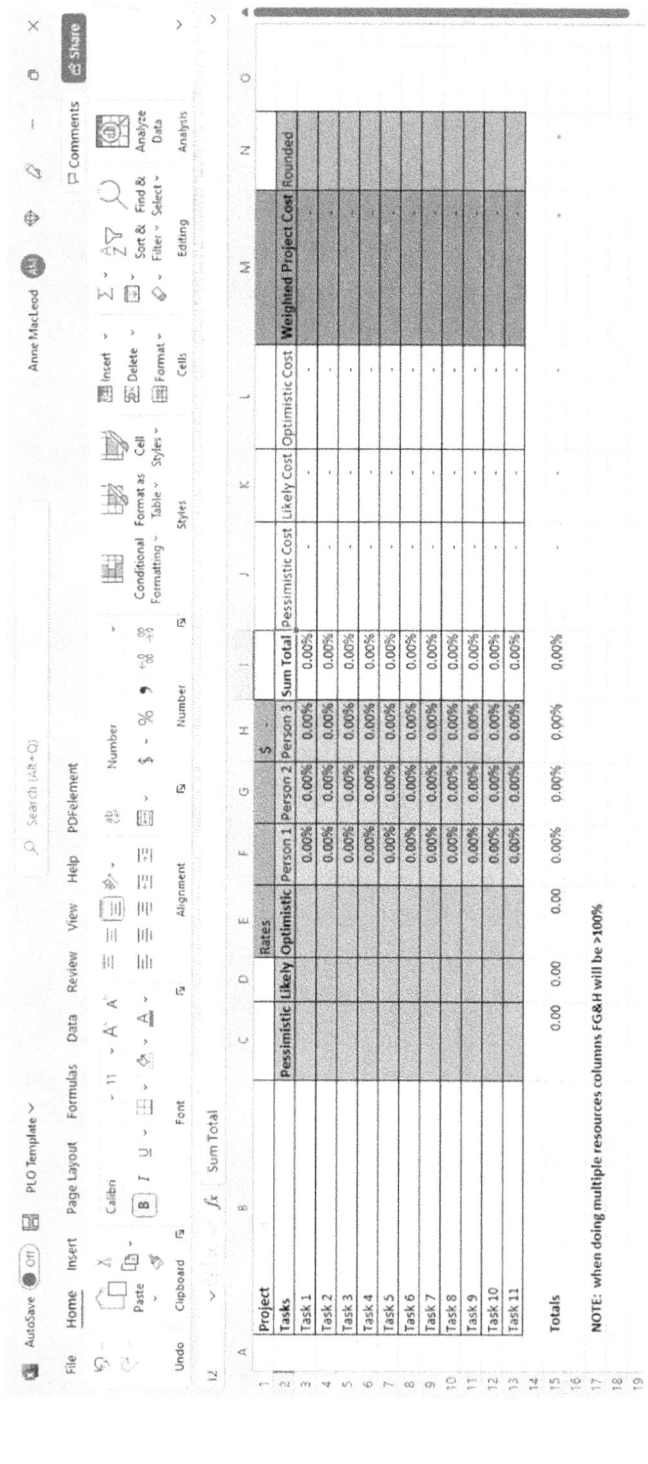

Figure 3.20 PLO template

organization gets the most value out of based on the types of projects you are delivering.

Key considerations about what models to use are:

- If your project is a pure software build or product development project, Agile is a good fit; however, if it involves modifying an existing system, or a substantial part of the project is not system related, again think of those construction projects; if any system projects involve installing third party software (buy instead of build), then the PMGB will be a better fit.
- If you are using user stories—regardless of the type of project—consider adding in the customer journey map; it can provide a better context to the user stories. Also, the customer journey map can ensure that you have the right user stories, from the right users.
- If the Agile project is large enough that you are using Epics to break down the work, then consider supplementing it with the project priority triangle (PPT) to ensure you align multiple teams to a common goal.
- Utilizing the planning backward techniques can substantially help you plan out sprints by identifying the pieces of work that can be best sequenced together to maximize the efficiency of testing and training. This combined with your user stories will help you come up with a great test plan for user acceptance testing and allow you to focus on smaller groups of users or test cases.

Overall, I recommend finding the methods that work best—deliver results—for your organization, your projects, and your customers and customize them to fit you. Then standardize and streamline them with a spirit of continuous improvement.

2.4 Quality & Risk

Quality

As with so many parts of the PMGB, this step relies on a key principle: customer first. The analogy I always use to describe quality is: think of quality-like specifications for cement; the specification for cement is readily understood and the measurement to that standard is robust and well understood. Cement is either good or bad.

The same is *not* true for software projects, service design, system implementations, and construction projects—whether they are residential, commercial, or industrial—that's where the challenge comes in. The quality standard and measurement to the standard are very much in the eye of the beholder. So, you need to make sure that you have the right eyes (customers) and the right beholding; the more you have the right people engaged to validate what you are delivering, the better your chances of success and being able to deliver a "quality" project.

For our quality specification and measurement to work, there are a couple of key strategies:

- Be clear about who your customer is—as we discussed in 2.2 People & Timeline. Further to that, you'll want to be clear about who the customer is for each deliverable—they will receive the output, ensure it meets their standards for quality, and then accept it. After that, they may add additional value to put it into its final form. See Figure 3.21.

  For example, in a software project, we may be delivering a project to build new functionality into a computer system that deals with transactions in the Customer Service Department; therefore, the customer of the project would be the CS Department. To build that software, we may need business analysts to develop user stories, developers to build the code, and testers to test the software. Each of these would be customers of each other. So, you end up with a chain of customers:

  So, each of these customers must do a quality review when they receive their deliverable and determine whether it meets their standards (you can see how consistently applied corporate standards could reduce the potential chaos around this conversation!) and either accept or reject it. Then they do their piece of value add to move things forward to the next customer with their project deliverable.

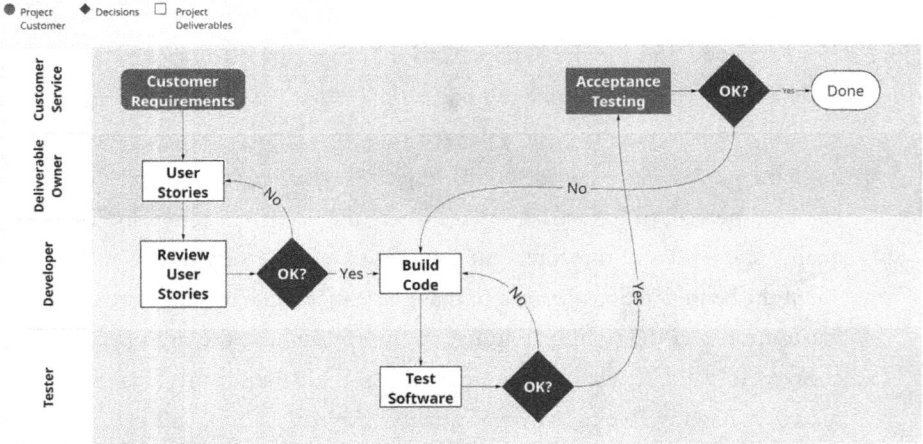

Figure 3.21 Software project process roles

Another pro tip is to have the customer as engaged as possible in each of these handoffs; you don't want to have to rework everything at the end. You want to ensure that your software build is aligned with their expectations along the way. More on that in the next chapter—Create.

- Another strategy I highly recommend is to negotiate at this stage of the project with the customer on the project acceptance criteria. What are the Must, Should, and Nice to Have elements that must be there to achieve the success criteria for the project? If you negotiate these criteria early in the planning stage and keep them up to date, you'll have a much clearer picture of where the finish line is. See Table 3.5 for definitions.

These two strategies will ensure that you keep your customer front and center as the project creates deliverables; also it aligns well with much of the work on minimum viable product for product startups and is of great help to projects intending to deliver results quickly.

Risk

I'm not going to spend much time on risk as this subject can be very broad and go very deep and I don't consider myself an expert. I'll quickly

Table 3.5 Project acceptance criteria definitions

Element	Definition	Completion Criteria
Must	Absolutely has to be delivered, otherwise the success criteria will not be achieved	100% must be delivered
Should	Negotiable within specific success criteria: These are things typically within parameters or quality specifications. That is, system response time must be less than one minute; however, it should be less than 10 seconds	Negotiate this threshold with the customer based on the PPT. If the priority is time, then very few of these will be delivered for the project to be complete
Nice to have	These are things, particularly in software projects, that we can "throw in" while we're in the neighborhood but weren't articulated in the scope as they weren't foreseen to directly contribute to project success criteria	Any of these that are delivered are gravy; there should be no commitment to these. However, the project team should get celebrated when they can go above and beyond and deliver these

go through a couple of great techniques that specifically relate to the PMGB and then recommend that you spend some time with Google or PMI if you're interested in pursuing it in more depth.

When we do PLOs in 2.2 People & Timeline, this exercise provides us with a unique ability to re-evaluate these estimates as they relate to risks. I've found that when people give you broad ranges, for example, an optimistic estimate of three days, likely of five days, and then pessimistic of three weeks, they are contemplating certain risks. So, for risks, go back to these estimates, look at the ones with wide ranges, and have the team clarify what they perceive as risks.

In addition to these risks there is a Miroverse template that walks you through a workshop specifically to develop risks and mitigations. This template can be found at www.miro.com/miroverse/risks-and-mitigations/.

2.5 Communication

When it comes to communication, there can never be enough plus it's complicated; that's why there is a step dedicated in this leg. This step intends to deal with the practical aspects of communication and to ensure you give communication its due when you're planning your project. If you want to formalize it into a communication plan document, there are tons of resources and templates on the Internet.

Things I do want you to consider when it comes to communication are:

- Use the knowledge of your team to determine your communication strategy; they know what works well or doesn't. You don't want to bring new technology or processes into your project that no one is familiar with! This will not help your communication be effective or sufficient. Also, remember for many pieces of communication, you may need to find ways to say it five to seven times in three different ways to be heard.
- Look for key project communications and have the team decide on the most appropriate methods, frequency, and format to utilize. At a minimum, these key project communications are:
  o *Project status*: Have a visual asynchronous way to provide this so that anyone can access on demand. Consider supplementing your project dashboard with a Loom video for key audiences that can be consumed on their schedule asynchronously. Give people the ability to comment or ask questions (more on asynchronous and synchronous a little later).
  o *Decisions*: These need to be communicated with at least the elements of what was decided, why, and the next steps or response to the decision. This is particularly important whether the decision is a yes or a no—people want to understand why or why not.
  o *Meeting outcomes*: This is a critical step, particularly for key meetings that involve decisions. I recommend adding a standard item to the agenda that ends the meeting with the communication messages from that meeting. Meetings with key stakeholders tend to have visibility in the organization and along with that go expectations—be

transparent about the reason for the meeting and the outcome.

- Wherever possible, leverage existing communication channels and processes for your project. For example, on an externally facing customer project, utilize whatever methods are already in place to communicate with customers, but be aware that as soon as you communicate to customers, you have raised expectations with them.

    In our customer care and billing project at a large Telco, we particularly considered the communication of a new billing format. We made the conscious decision to not tell customers their bill was going to change but focused on communicating when the new bill went out and the features and benefits of the new format. We didn't want people holding onto their bills to compare them to the new ones when they came out, as certain system constraints meant some presentation elements would be lost in the new version. We overcompensated in communication materials and staff to be able to explain the new bills and had positive feedback from customers.

- If you have the opportunity (usually if your project has enough profile or budget), I highly recommend having a communication resource assigned at least part-time to the project. This is particularly important if you are going to use a variety of communication channels with different stakeholder groups: managing Facebook, Twitter, and website copy—it's a big job and needs to be resourced appropriately.

- Check in with the team and your stakeholders on what is working and what isn't in your communications; do retrospectives, surveys, or whatever is necessary to get feedback.

If you have a distributed team, there are several considerations you'll want to incorporate in your communication plans. Be visual about everything you can; supplement your task management view with a virtual space. This is where Miro is particularly helpful, and you'll want to incorporate:

- Shared team space that provides one source of truth. It can include all the project documents or links to them. It allows everyone access to the same information.
- The space should provide some personal space to allow for the team to interact, share stories and anecdotes about their personal life, and reflect the project culture.
- It should have some messy space—areas for the groups to brainstorm, ideate, problem solve, and be creative. Balance this with some good visual structure and wayfinding, so people can navigate easily through the space.

Asynchronous Versus Synchronous Communication

Our distributed teams' meetings have become synonymous with communication; however, this isn't always the best use of people's time and if your team crosses multiple time zones, it can be downright difficult. To reduce the number of meetings or at least make them more focused on key collaborative tasks and workshops, consider moving as much content as you can to asynchronous. That way, people can consume it in their own time and pace and even contribute to the preparation for a meeting. Table 3.6 contains some ideas.

Table 3.6 Meetings and asynchronous methods

Meeting	Asynchronous alternative	Consideration
Project status report	Miro Board with TalkTrack	• Find a way to ensure you can get feedback from those who view the video, by commenting • Ensure that you monitor the usage of it—if no one is watching, it's not working!! Find out why and fix it
Retrospective brainstorming	Miro Board with TalkTrack	Save your group time for synthesizing feedback, getting to the root cause of issues, and developing action plans

Meeting	Asynchronous alternative	Consideration
Beers after work	Have a team sharing space on a Miro Board—places to add personal photos, favorite shows, must-see movies, and book reviews	The trick here is to be creative and don't have this as a one-time activity; find ways to revisit and update this space regularly
Premeeting material	Documents shared before the meeting—even a Loom video of them	To make meetings as focused as possible on solving a problem or making a decision, try sending out materials or briefing notes before the meeting. Also, recognize that folks may not have time to review them before the meeting, so have a contingency plan

Understand Go/No Go & Learn

Critical at the conclusion of this phase is a Go/No Go decision on whether the project should proceed—far too many projects keep blasting along without touching this base!

It's now time to compare the key elements of your Listen leg to the results of your Understand leg: What do you know now that you didn't before? Is the viable idea a viable project? Has anything changed in terms of key components, priorities, and success criteria? Also, it is critical to revisit the external drivers that affect the organization and could affect the project—look around at market shifts, technology changes, corporate priority changes, resource constraints, funding shifts, and competitive influences. Finally, by setting the decision up this way, you can summarize all the good work that has gone into the project so far. If the decision is not to proceed—at this time—then the work done to date can be neatly packaged up and the project paused and revisited at a more appropriate time. Don't forget that you've done the work on the Listen leg to ensure that it's aligned corporately, so this project is still a good idea, barring significant shifts in corporate strategy. It will be so much easier for the next team to pick up where you've left off and reuse the knowledge already developed.

To facilitate this meeting, I've prepared a 3P meeting agenda that looks like this.

Purpose: Why are we having this meeting? To decide whether this project should proceed to Create.

Process: What process are we going to use to arrive at the payoff?

1. Review the PPT and the proposed timeline: Do they align?
2. Review the project success criteria and the resource plan and deliverables: Do they align?
3. Review the project budget and resource requirements: Do these align?
4. Review the project portfolio and see if anything has changed on the PICK chart.
5. Any external considerations on whether we should proceed— market shifts, technology changes, corporate priority changes, resource constraints, and competitive influences.
6. Gather feedback and decide whether to proceed utilizing the pros and cons template.
7. Determine the communication messages and audience for the decision.

Payoff: To decide whether our viable idea is a viable project that should proceed at this time.

When you're preparing for the meeting, you could end up with a board that kind of looks like the one shown in Figure 3.22.

What we want to do is ensure that our outputs from Listen—the PPT and the success criteria still align. So, let's start with our three PPT scenarios and what we are checking or looking for in terms of alignment.

In the case of a time scope priority (Figure 3.23), you'll want to see a range in the project budget and deliverables that closely align with the success criteria. You want deliverables that are clearly scoped and readily measured to quality and customer expectations. Also, the timeline needs to align with the duration expectations of the decision makers, your sponsor, and your customer.

In the case of a scope/cost priority (Figure 3.24) and having a limited budget, you want to see a very narrow range on the budget estimate and again very specific deliverables and scope of work that is readily understood by customers. Then it will be either a very limited resource plan

Understand Go/No Go

Project timeline reflects project priorities

Project deliverables align with success criteria

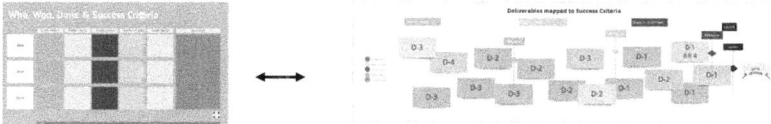

Resource strategy aligns with resource plan

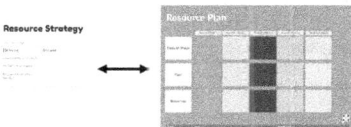

PLO aligns with project priorities

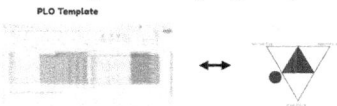

Project Portfolio Review

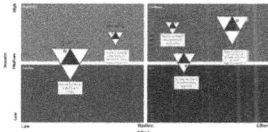

Figure 3.22 Understand Go/No Go

(you don't have the budget for resources) or it could be that the resources will only be working part-time, which will show up in the PLO.

For our third scenario with a time cost constraint (Figure 3.25), we want to see very narrow PLOs in our budget and a launch date or project duration that aligns with our need to meet the timeline. Again, the scope will need to be clear and readily understood in terms of quality. I find, with this scenario, the timeline for the project should be 90 to 120 days; this will ensure that the scope is specific and the budget is met. The deliverables should be unambiguous—you don't want to see anything that refers to building a plan, doing research, or market testing.

Minimize Time   **Maximize Scope**

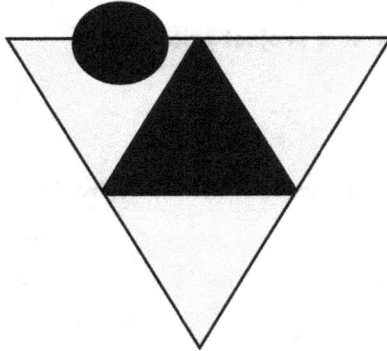

Minimize Cost

We will spend money to ensure we meet our scope
and timeline

Figure 3.23 Understand alignment scenario 1

Minimize Time   **Maximize Scope**

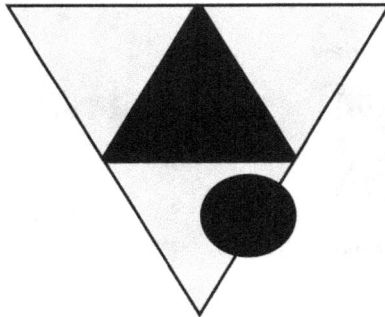

Minimize Cost

We will take the time within our limited budget to
achieve this specific scope

Figure 3.24 Understand alignment scenario 2

Who Should Attend This Meeting?

This meeting needs to be about deciding and looking for the authority, responsibility, and accountability for that decision. Also, it needs to
be fully supported by the project team. I would recommend that each

Minimize Time   **Maximize Scope**

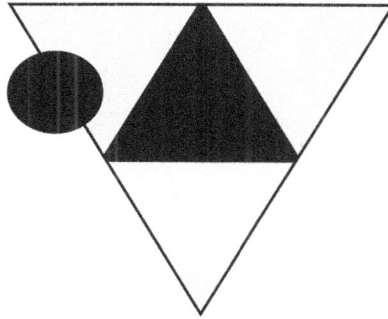

Minimize Cost

We will sacrifice scope to meet our timeline and budget

Figure 3.25 Understand alignment scenario 3

project team member be represented at the meeting—there may be questions about the scope and resourcing they can answer in the meeting. The decision makers for the meeting must be the customer and the sponsor, but could also include senior managers who are responsible for either processes or objectives that this project supports.

Making the Decision in the Meeting

I'm going to recommend the pros and cons combined with a double voting technique to make this decision. See Chapter 4—3.5 Make Decisions for the details. You'll be using a board that looks like the one shown in Figure 3.26. This template is available as a pdf at www.pmgameboard .com/shop/delphi-decision-template/ and as a Miroverse template at www.miro.com/miroverse/pmgb-decision-template/.

Finally, don't forget to conclude the meeting with your communication plan for the decision—whichever way it goes!

Understand Retrospectives

The focus of the retrospective in this leg is to ensure that the team is applying the team norms they set out in the project kickoff as well as

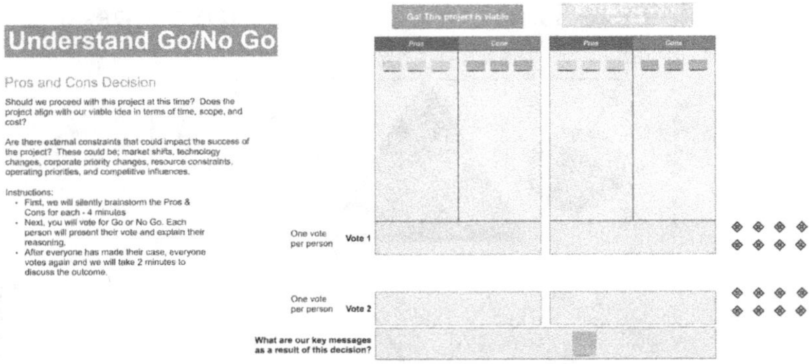

Figure 3.26 Understand Go/No Go decision

improve our project planning processes for future projects. As these are two vastly different focuses, I recommend doing the retrospective in two different meetings. Also, I think as we are still early in the process of building relationships in the project team, I also encourage teams to do these in a meeting as opposed to asynchronously. When the team gets into a rhythm of doing retros, you can move to asynchronous—at a minimum for the gathering issues and opportunities for improvement.

See Chapter 5—4.2 Retrospectives—for more details on retrospectives.

Guess what! I've prepared a couple of proposed 3P agendas for each of these meetings!

Team Norms Retrospective

Purpose: Why are we having this meeting? To ensure our team norms are working as intended.

Process: What is the process we will use to achieve the payoff?

1. Icebreaker activity.
2. Review the team norms developed as part of your project kickoff.
3. Silent brainstorm what's working well for each norm.
4. Have everyone group the ideas into common themes.
5. For each of them, develop a plan to reinforce or continue this success. Consider how we get new team members onboard and how we celebrate these successes.
6. Silent brainstorm what's not working for each norm.

7. Have everyone group the ideas into common themes.
8. Do some root cause analysis on why this isn't working; use five whys if appropriate.
9. Develop an action plan—with due dates, resources assigned, and follow-up activities to address these issues.
10. Determine the communication messages from this retrospective.

Payoff: Ensuring our team norms are relevant and continuously improved.

By gathering feedback on how the team is performing, we can rectify issues before the more intense work in the next leg!

Understand Retrospective

Our second way of continuously improving or learning is to do a retrospective on the Understand phase itself. We want to ensure that we are continually improving our planning for future projects and improving the project maturity practices in the organization.

The proposed agenda for this retrospective is as follows.

Purpose: Why are we having this meeting? To ensure our project planning process is working well.

Process: What is the process we will use to achieve the payoff?
1. Icebreaker activity.
2. Review the key dates and activities completed in this leg:
   o Project Kickoff meeting
   o 2.1 Scope of Work
   o 2.2 People & Timeline
   o 2.3 Budget & Equipment
   o 2.4 Quality & Risk
3. Silent brainstorm what's working well for planning overall.
4. Have everyone group the ideas into common themes.
5. For each of them, develop a plan to reinforce or continue this success. Consider templates, processes, and how we reinforce these successful practices.
6. Silent brainstorm what's not working for each activity.
7. Have everyone group the ideas into common themes.

8. Do some root cause analysis on why this isn't working; use five whys if appropriate.

9. Develop an action plan—with due dates, resources assigned, and follow-up activities to address these issues.

10. Determine the communication messages from this retrospective.

Payoff: Ensuring that our planning process is continuously improved.

In Summary

You made it through the second leg! Congratulations! At the conclusion of this leg, you should have the information to ensure that your team has a plan they understand and support and is achievable. Your customer, sponsor, and key stakeholders have reassurances that the outcomes they are looking for can be achieved for the time and resources expended.

It is important to remember that PMI recommends that, in terms of effort, you should spend 20 to 30 percent on planning (which would be our Listen + Understand legs) and 5 to 10 percent on closing (our Reflect) so that means 60 to 75 percent of your efforts is in the next leg—Create. This is another reason we emphasize selecting the appropriate collaboration techniques that are going to get you the best results in your project planning.

Congrats, you've completed another leg and you have a project plan!

CHAPTER 4

Create—Delivering Value

Overview

This is the leg where all the action happens; it's also where the most effort is expended—remember 20 to 30 percent to initiate, 5 to 10 percent to close, so 60 to 75 percent to create. For this leg of the Project Management GameBoard (PMGB), the focus is on managing expectations, risks, and changes while keeping our team resilient, responsive, and operating at peak performance through collaboration.

From a collaboration perspective, this leg involves harnessing the team's knowledge, expertise, and authority to:

- Agree on key dates.
- Tools to support the project and collaborate.
- Identify project risks and mitigations.
- Manage change requests.
- Support the decision-making process and collaborate with the project sponsor and customer.

Finally, in this leg, we'll explore what I think are some best practices or considerations for the selection and setup of your project management system of choice, but you'll have to figure out what tech works best for you and your team!

In summary, the Create leg looks like Figure 4.1 from an interaction perspective.

It's important to keep this figure in mind as we go through each step in this leg as there are a lot of interactions between steps; many of them focused on managing stakeholders' expectations as we deliver the project.

The Create leg of the PMGB is the one leg where most of my clients do a great job. This is often true because good people make up for bad processes! The considerations, techniques, tools, and templates I cover will be for you to supplement your existing practices or to add collaboration.

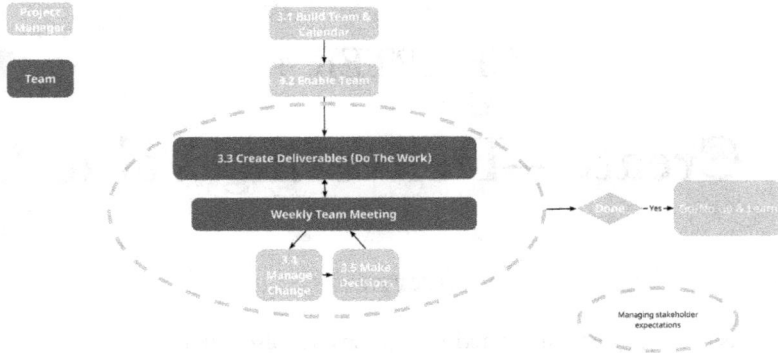

Figure 4.1 Create interactions

For this leg (see Figure 4.2), we have:

- 3.1 Build Team: This is the onboarding of our delivery team and agreeing on our weekly team schedule, reporting, and communication tools. Also, we'll workshop our project plan into an implementation plan with dates and resources assigned to translate into our PM tool of choice.
- 3.2 Enable Team: This step takes what we've agreed to earlier and highlights the support the project manager provides to team members, the project sponsor, and the customer. We'll cover establishing authority levels for the team, the sponsor, and the customer.
- 3.3 Create Deliverables: This is where the work is done by the team, the weekly project status meeting, and finally in-depth team pulse checks to ensure we are sustaining our team culture.
- 3.4 Managing Change: The process of assessing the project impact, deciding whether to proceed with the change, and negotiating changes with stakeholders.
- 3.5 Making Decisions: Getting the right people in the room, framing the decision, collaborative techniques to make decisions effectively and efficiently, and communicating those decisions and next steps.
- Go/No Go & Learn: Completion criteria and retrospectives.

Figure 4.2 PMGB Create

3.1 Build Team & Calendar

This step is all about moving from planning to implementation. Critical to that success are three things:

- Onboarding new resources that may not have been involved in planning the project, having the team understand our team norms, and setting the team up for success by agreeing on the tools to be used for project tracking and communicating.
- Assigning dates and names to our planned project deliverables. We'll do this through a collaborative workshop that will ensure everyone is clear about their responsibilities as well as their dependencies on others.

- Finally, some tips and tricks on how to set up your project task management system successfully—that aligns with our success criteria and incorporates deliverables to owners and customers.

To accomplish all this, we have two workshops: the team project kickoff and the key dates and accountabilities workshop.

Here's a proposed agenda for the Create Project Kickoff workshop.

Purpose: Why are we having this meeting? To build relationships and understand roles and responsibilities, processes, and project tools.

Process: What is the process we are going to use to arrive at the payoff?

1. Expectations and concerns.
2. Welcome!
   o Sponsor introduction.
   o Project customer introduction.
   o Review of Listen and Understand outputs.
   o Review of team norms.
3. Discussion and decision on tools and techniques to be used to communicate and track the project.
4. Assign dates and names to our plan.
5. Review of our roles and responsibilities (update the RACI).
6. Set up our weekly meeting:
   o Review our weekly meeting agenda.
   o Determine weekly date and time.
   o Agree on a format for attendance and substitutions (record meetings, allow representatives to attend, other?).

Payoff: We understand our roles in the project, processes, and tools to support the project and the team.

Considerations for this meeting:

- Overall: This meeting is a great opportunity to introduce and onboard any resources acquired through your procurement process. Reviewing team norms and the outputs from the Understand leg may be appropriate in the meeting when there is a significant change in resources from the planning phase or one-on-one with specific resources depending on the time available and their experience with projects or this project. You may want to split this agenda into two meetings. If the project tool choice is a protracted discussion, then make this a separate meeting to abide by our two-hour meeting rule.

- Sponsor and customer introduction: This is a great way to get them engaged in the project and to have them articulate their vision of the project to the delivery team in their own words. It also helps the project team have visibility to these key stakeholders.
- Listen and Understand outputs: I recommend, at an absolute minimum, you cover the project priority triangle and the project success criteria and answer any questions the team has.
- Tools and techniques to be used to communicate and track the project: If you are in the business of delivering projects, this may be obvious as you will probably have standards and the same tool for every project. See the expanded discussion later for further considerations.
- Set up our weekly meeting: Set a regular day of the week and a regular time. Doing this will increase the likelihood that people will be able to attend as they will start scheduling the rest of their workload around that time. This also helps you get into a regular cadence for reporting and tracking; people will be able to know their deadlines and forecast future work. A suggested agenda is provided.

Tools for Tracking Project Status

Let's briefly expand on some key concepts that align with the PMGB that you will want to consider for your project tools:

- Use the project tracking tool with the most—broadest adoption—within the team. Don't ask the entire team to adopt a new tool they've never used just because the PM likes it or has heard good things about it! If the bulk of the team is comfortable with MS Excel or Google Sheets, find a way to make it work. This is particularly important to ensure that the PM doesn't become the "owner" of inputting all the data and that team members take responsibility for their work.

- Use the collaboration tools that the team has the most experience with and that best complements your project tracking tool. During this leg of the project, you'll be collaborating in weekly meetings to understand where you are and where you're going. You'll also be collaborating when deliberating on change requests, making project decisions, and doing team pulse checks and retrospectives. I recommend Miro!

- You want to be able to do traceability of your scope from the success criteria, key deliverables, and/or critical path in the Understand leg through the delivery or Create leg. When configuring your system, consider using tags to trace success criteria and priorities for critical path elements.

- Ensure that you have a calendar and Gantt view of the project. People think in calendars, so this will be critical for the weekly status meetings. The Gantt view is most helpful for doing visual checks on interdependencies, overlaps, and handoffs between resources and teams. Being able to share these views in team meetings and when collaborating on your next steps is critical.

- Talk about what works well for team messaging—if you use Slack corporately, talk through some team norms around its use, be clear on who's the administrator, and talk through the channels you want to adopt.

3.2 Enable Team

This step focuses on how the project manager provides support to team members, the project sponsor, and the customer. To be effective collaborators, the team, project sponsor, and customer need to understand their roles and responsibilities and have the processes to support them. These consist of:

- Team members: Understanding deadlines, their contribution or scope of work (how their expertise is to be utilized), providing feedback on the quality of their inputs, and contributing their expertise to problem solving and key decisions. Team members will ideally have participated in the planning of the project from our work in the Understand leg, so we'll focus on enabling them to contribute to team meetings and project status.
- Project sponsor: Their primary collaboration role is in managing change requests and decision making. They are also responsible for being the project team's eyes and ears to operational and strategic issues that could impact the project and a communication channel to their peers.
- Project customer: Their primary collaboration role is also in managing change requests and decision making; however, they also have a responsibility to inform the project team of operational issues that could impact the project.

Supporting the Team

As mentioned previously, this is all about enabling team members to participate effectively in key collaboration activities of team meetings, change requests, and project decision making. The latter two are covered in steps 3.4 Managing Change and 3.5 Making Decisions, so I'll focus on enabling team members.

I've found that team members have a wide variety of ways to work and manage their work. It's the project manager's job to work with them to find the most effective way for the team member to work and not impose their methods on the team member. They may need some coaching to find tools to prioritize tasks, delegate where appropriate, monitor, and adjust. The project manager is a subject manager expert on exactly these types of activities and can suggest tools and techniques and coach team members to improve their skills and make them effective. With these skills, the collaboration in our weekly project status meetings will keep the whole team on track.

Supporting the Project Sponsor and Customer

In 3.1 Build Team & Calendar, we created the dates and finalized the deliverables and resources for the project, so we're now ready to talk specifics with the project sponsor and customer about the project team's authorities.

> *Purpose*: Why are we having this meeting? To validate and customize the processes and authorities for the project sponsor and project customer.
>
> *Process*: What is the process we are going to use to arrive at the payoff?
> 1. Expectations and concerns.
> 2. Walkthrough and feedback on the project schedule.
> 3. Discussion of tools to be used to track and communicate our overall project status.
> 4. Review the change process and agree on our authority levels and change thresholds.
>
> *Payoff*: The project sponsor and project customer are comfortable with the timeline, scope, and budget detailed by the project team. The decision authorities and process are clear for the project.

Here are some considerations for parts of the meeting:

- Project tracking and communication tools. These folks have specific needs and expectations—inviting them to the project Slack channel will not suffice to understand the project status. You'll want to establish asynchronous information they can access as well as specific ways for them to provide feedback and input. This information must be comprehensive about time, scope, and cost and timely. At a minimum, schedule regular one-on-one meetings to address their viewpoints, solicit information from them, and stay in touch.

- Change processes need to deal with time, scope, and cost and establish thresholds for each element. For example, if you have a project with an 18-month schedule, you may set a threshold of escalating any change that results in more than a two-week delay, but also give the project team latitude to spend up to $x,xxx dollars to deal with changes that improve scope delivery and don't affect the timeline.

3.3 Create Deliverables

This step is all about the interactions of doing the work and our weekly team meeting—remember the image in Figure 4.2. See Figure 4.3.

This is also reinforced with the circle on the PMGB. It's all about managing stakeholder expectations as our project progresses. As we deliver our project, we may encounter issues that require change requests or decisions to be made. We want to do all these activities in the most collaborative way possible as that will keep all our stakeholders aligned and the project team moving forward. Critical to the success of this step will be to have collaborative weekly status meetings and team pulse checks to ensure our project culture is resilient.

Weekly Project Status Meetings

To make these as collaborative as possible, we want to focus on problem solving; so the first part of our meeting is focused on understanding

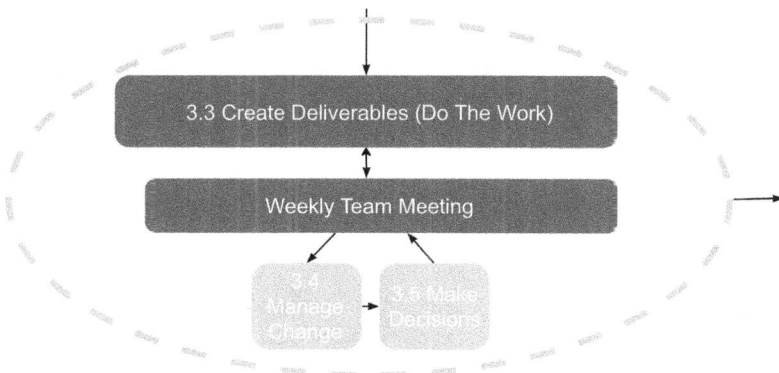

Figure 4.3 Create interaction details

where there may be problems and the second part on resolving those issues with activities around root cause, solution evaluation, and then the outputs of our action plan and communication plan.

> *Purpose*: Why are we having this meeting? To understand the status of our project and resolve any issues.
>
> *Process*: What is the process we are going to use to arrive at the payoff?
> - Are there any issues with our key dates?
> - Are there any issues with our inputs: delays or quality received?
> - Are there any issues with our outputs: delays or quality?
> - How do we fix those problems?
>   o Root cause.
>   o Solution evaluation.
>   o In scope or escalate?
>   o Action plan.
>   o Communication plan.
> - What has been delivered this week—celebrate success.
>
> *Payoff*: The team agrees on the project status and has resolved any issues with time, budget, or scope. Issues that aren't resolved are understood and can be escalated to the project sponsor and customer.

Let's explore some of these in more detail:

- Overall: If you consistently use this agenda, people will learn to come prepared. The first few meetings may take one to two hours, but once your team gets into a rhythm and gets traction, you should be able to get these down to a half hour!
- Root cause: You'll want to consider using five whys if the reasons for the issue aren't obvious.

Five Whys

It can help uncover what is going on, prevent symptoms, and potentially identify stakeholders or gaps in the project. There is a Miroverse template that can be found at www.miro.com/miroverse/root-cause-analysis-the-five-whys/. See Figure 4.4.

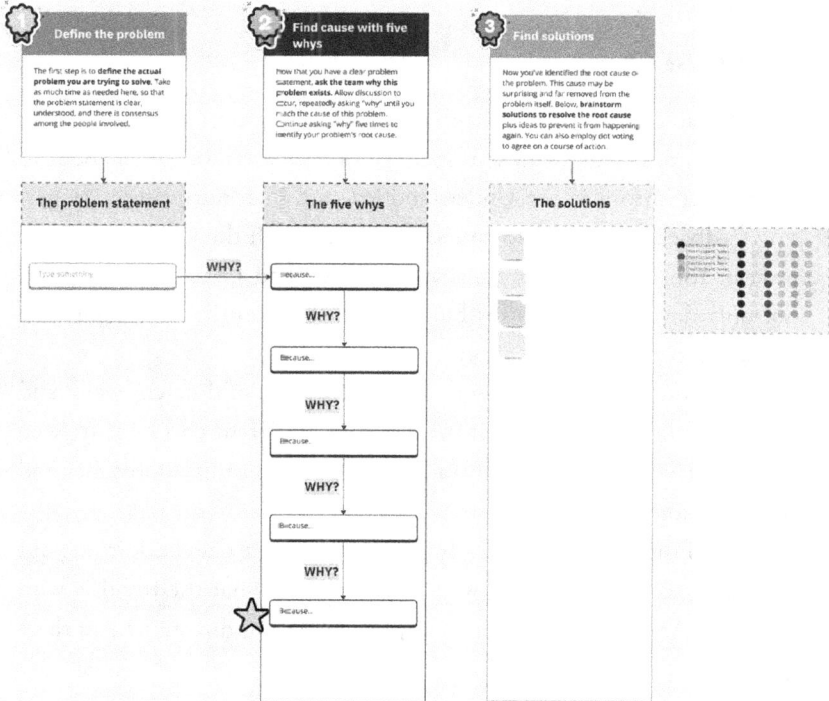

Figure 4.4 Five whys template

- Solution evaluation: The key collaboration piece of this step is to ensure that you hear from everyone on the project team and not just the loudest voice in the room or the person with the most senior title. To keep this simple, I would recommend ensuring you have each team member speak to the proposed solution before reaching a consensus. If you want some more structured and specific techniques, check out those in 3.4 Manage Change and 3.5 Make Decisions.
- Scope or escalate is pretty straightforward: If it's within the team's authority, the team adjusts the project accordingly and

proceeds to implement the solution. If it exceeds their authority, then it will be escalated to the project sponsor and customer.

- Action plan: This includes who is doing what and by when.
- Communication plan: I always advocate touching this base. Which stakeholders should we be informing about our resolution? Are there lessons learned for other project teams? Who needs to know or could benefit from how we solve this issue?

Team Pulse Checks

Part of enabling the team is ensuring we are paying close attention to our team culture, starting with setting it up for success as we talked about in our project kickoff in the Understand leg, and then nurturing it by getting feedback and acting to course correct through the Create leg of the project. You'll remember from that section we had space for the team to not only develop their norms but also possibly identify hard skills, soft skills, and personal information.

To do our pulse checks, you can do it a couple of different ways, and I would recommend mixing it up and doing different check-ins to keep the feedback fresh and thoughtful. Table 4.1 gives some approaches and considerations.

Any of these methods will allow you to get some data back from your team and, as the PM, you'll want to determine what the trend is with this data. Are things going gradually in the wrong direction? Are there

Table 4.1 Project stages and team pulse checks

Project Stage	Approach	Consideration
Early in the Create stage	Get feedback through an anonymous survey	When the team is new, they may be reluctant to share, particularly if some bad behaviors are showing up in the team
Any stage, but you've noticed the culture deteriorating	Retrospective framed by the project norms	The big question is whether to do this anonymously or collectively—that depends on the dynamics of the team as well as the culture of the organization. If you have a strong (well-defined), resilient, and open culture, then don't hesitate to do it collectively. If your organization has no stated values, is competitive, and is defensive, then I would recommend doing the brainstorming portion asynchronously and then work with the team to group them and do a thorough root cause analysis and to determine corrective actions

Project Stage	Approach	Consideration
Any stage, but you've not checked in for a while	Pick one of the norms and ask team members for stories where that was demonstrated	For teams who've not yet gone through storming and norming, you may want to use this as a reason to celebrate. Capturing and sharing these types of experiences is a great validation of the team walking the talk and is a great way to onboard new resources to what we mean by a particular norm
Any stage	Sentiment analysis based on your project norms	This can be a way to mix it up and solicit feedback. Using emojis is fast, easily understood, and visual

particular problem areas that are recurring? Does it warrant a deeper dive into the root causes or even an escalation to the project sponsor and project customer?

For a template and more tips, check Reflect—4.2 Retrospectives.

But don't forget, at the end of the day, you and your project can only achieve so much if the corporate culture isn't supportive of this type of team support. If so, that might be the time to start polishing your resume if you find you're pushing rope!

3.4 Managing Change

It's not if things change; it's when things change! One of the keys to success at this stage of any project is being able to respond to and negotiate change requests. I've found that many organizations are afraid of change requests and will go to almost any lengths to avoid them as they are perceived as problems. Change requests are never problems; they are always opportunities to respond to stakeholders' needs and to be responsive within the project to changing circumstances.

So now that we've accepted that change is a part of managing our project and adopted the philosophy that we are going to be responsive to our customers, let's understand the key elements of managing it:

- The process: a generic process to follow.
- Collaborative tools or techniques to support the process: some we've already covered like our project priority triangle, five whys, and PLOs plus additional ones like the Fishbone. Specifically for change requests, we pull some of these together differently.

Change Request Process

I have developed a simple but effective process illustrated by Figure 4.5.

There is a PDF version of this diagram available at www.pmgameboard .com/product/project-change-request-process-template/.

Let's review each step:

- Idea/issue: Anyone can have an idea for a change—customers need to identify ideas for change—and note that these can be internal or external customers. The key to the success of this step is to have an intake form that is easily accessible and has some prescriptive or mandatory fields so that the PM and the team can move the change through the process as quickly as possible.

  Also, you want to ensure you're asking some probing questions to ensure you're getting thoughtful changes and not just spur-of-the-moment ideas or whims. Questions that ask about the impact of the requested change are helpful, such as what would be the benefit of this change, what are the implications if it isn't implemented, and what is the impact on resources in your department/team?

  For issues, these will typically come from your weekly project status meeting for items that are too complicated for the team to resolve in that meeting. You can also have ideas or issues coming from the project sponsor, customer, or external stakeholders.

- Triage: This needs to be done initially by the PM and then reviewed by the project team and should include:
  - A category for the change. I've provided a few generic suggestions, but use categories that are meaningful to your organization. Particularly consider ensuring there are less than seven categories and that they mean something when people are initiating changes and to the team when reviewing changes as well as periodically reviewing changes after a project or in a retrospective to be able to identify trends. Some suggested basic categories are:
    - Defect: Something that has been delivered by the project team that isn't working properly.

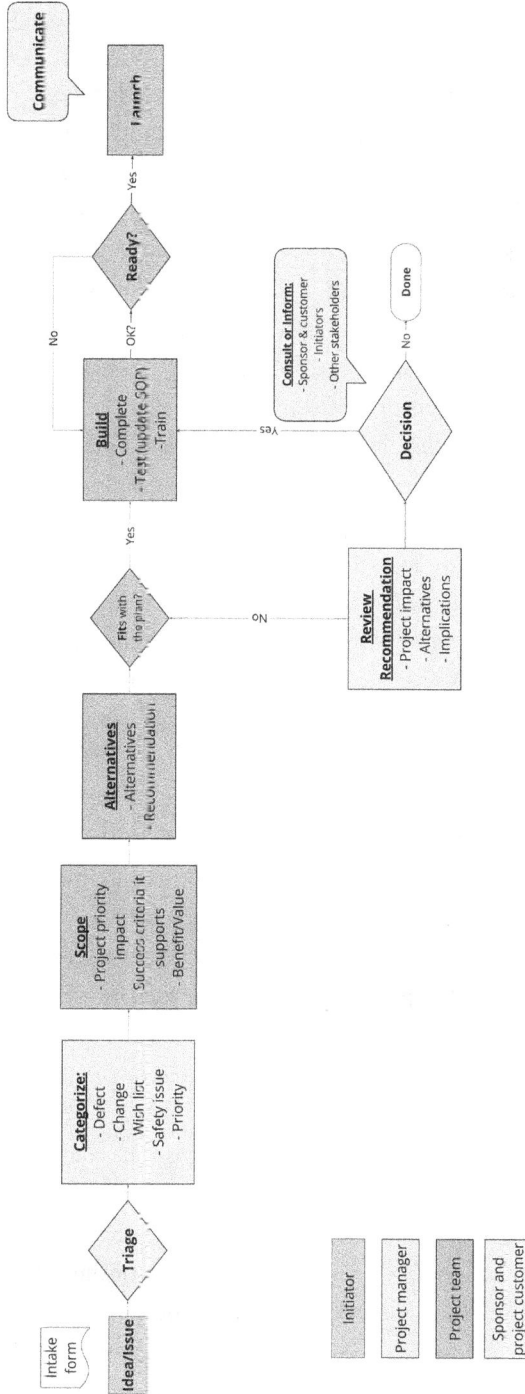

Figure 4.5 Change process

- Change: Just the way it sounds—a scope, time, budget, or resource change.
- Wish list: Future opportunity, particularly true in multiphased projects; this category works well to keep track of future phase ideas or as an input to your backlog.
- Safety issue: These are mandatory things, non-negotiable changes. In many organizations, safety is one of those categories; I've also seen people use legislation as a category for changes that have come from external organizations, for example, change the tax rate on all our products or services.
  o Priority: At the triage stage, I would recommend starting with low, medium, and high and then refining the priority as the change is reviewed with the team. I've often seen teams have a reprioritization once the change is scoped.
- Scope: This will be in terms of benefit or value to the project as well as project impact. Note that you will be developing this with the project team and potentially could require circling back with the initiator to ensure your team properly understands the change.

  You'll want to include which project success criteria this supports. Also, this scope statement should be comprehensive enough for the team to be able to estimate the time and effort required to complete and the potential benefit to be realized.

  Project impact is in terms of schedule, resources required, budget, as well as the impact on the project priority triangle. To understand the impact of the requested change, you can use five whys or the fishbone diagram to scope the change See Table 4.2.
- Alternatives: In this portion of the discussion, you are looking to solicit the expertise of the team to either resolve the issue or alternatives to deliver on the idea. You'll want to select the tools or techniques that best match the size of the issue to be resolved. If you want to keep it simple for a small change, use brainwriting; for more extensive changes, use the PLOs and critical path. In all cases, you'll want to use the PICK chart to

Table 4.2 Approaches to analyze change requests

Approach	Format	Consideration
Five whys	Root cause analysis	This technique can ensure that the project team is not addressing a symptom, but the root cause of the issue or change identified. A Miro template is available at www.miro.com/miroverse/root-cause-analysis-the-five-whys/
Fishbone diagram	A method to understand the scope of the alternatives or root cause analysis	This technique can ensure the team fully understands the scope of the issue or the scope of the actions to correct the issue. A Miro template is available at www.miro.com/miroverse/fishbone-rca-template/

gather input from the team on the impact of the alternatives. See Table 4.3.

- Fits with the plan? This is the team decision point; we take the information we gathered about the impact and compare it to the project priority triangle and success criteria. If the change doesn't significantly alter these, then the team needs to note the change and proceed to build.

Don't forget that we negotiated project team authority limits in the second step of this leg (3.2 Enable Team), so if it's within our authority, we want to proceed as quickly as possible. However, if it exceeds the limits of our authority, it will need to be escalated to the project sponsor and project customer.

Table 4.3 Tools to analyze alternatives

Brainwriting	A type of brainstorming to assess alternatives	Helpful when you are trying to understand the implications of a change and solicit input from the entire team or specialists within the team
PLOs	Collaborative estimating	Having the team complete PLOs will ensure that we understand the implications of the change in terms of resourcing, effort, and elapsed time required to complete the change
Critical path	Timeline or schedule	This can be helpful to get the team to think through the key steps and provide updates to your project schedule
PICK chart	Decision support tool	Helps us weigh alternatives to ensure the approach to the change delivers the most value to the project

- Recommendation to project sponsor and customer: This is exactly how it sounds; we have the project team prepare the recommendation as mentioned earlier and then arrange a meeting with the project sponsor and customer. I'll go through the details of that meeting in the Negotiating Changes section.
- Build, ready, and launch: Again just the way it sounds; once the change has been approved, we build/create it, including testing or training as appropriate. Then we launch the change.
- Communication: There are a couple of key communication opportunities in this process. They are:
  o When a request is received, there needs to be an acknowledgment—even if it's automated back to the initiator so that they know it's in the pipeline.
  o The change needs to be tracked through its life cycle so the project team can communicate the status or so that initiators and other stakeholders can understand the status of their requests.
  o Whether the project team or the sponsor and customer decide to proceed or not, this needs to be clearly communicated, particularly to the initiator, and when the change is not moving forward, the reasons why.
  o Finally, we need to communicate when changes are anticipated to be launched to those impacted by the change. For example, if the people impacted have been involved in training for the change, then communication of the anticipated launch is most appropriate. If the change doesn't require formal training to be completed, then the communication of the launch may need to be more robust to ensure that those impacted understand the change and don't get surprised!

Change Workshop

In summary, you'll want to consider all the aforementioned and build a workshop, and the Miro board would look something like in Figure 4.6.

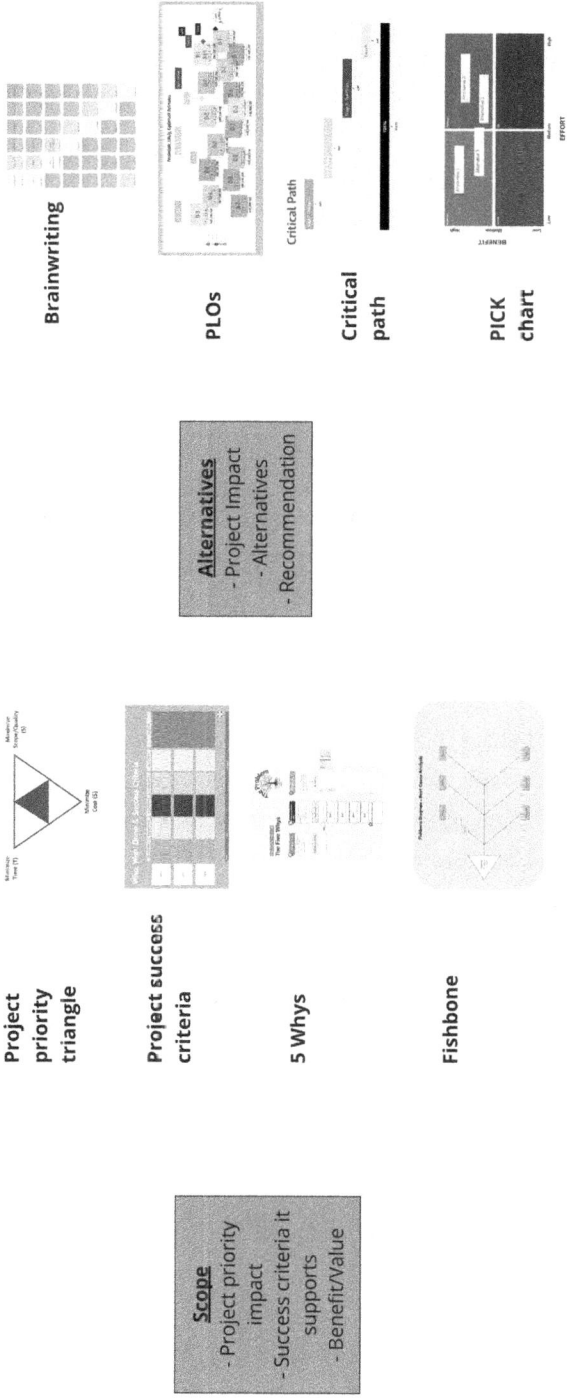

Figure 4.6 Change workshop

This will allow your team to review the material and scope of the change and then to work through alternatives and either implement the change if it's within their authority or make a recommendation to the project sponsor and customer.

Fishbone Root Cause Analysis

This is another tool that can help with root cause analysis and is particularly helpful when scoping a project change. It ensures that the team has considered multiple facets of the scope. See Figure 4.7. There is a template available in the Miroverse at www.miro.com/miroverse/fishbone-rca-template/. There is a PDF version available at www.pmgameboard .com/shop/rca-fishbone-template/.

Check out the link for resources and details about how to use the fishbone most effectively: www.lean-manufacturing-junction.com/2019/ 11/types-of-fishbone-diagrams/.

Negotiating Changes

While there are changes that will not impact the project scope, budget, or timeline materially and be pushed through by the project team, there is a significant chance some will require you to negotiate with the project sponsor and/or customer. There are some different nuances based on these different stakeholders.

> *Customers*: In many cases, there will be dependencies with customers to complete key project deliverables; there are usually two types that cause project delays:

- You are waiting for customers to provide key content.
- Customers don't make decisions in a timely fashion.

I've found that, with customer delays, the key is ensuring they clearly understand their responsibilities and the timelines. In the first case, you will need to ensure that the customer understands not only the content expected from them but also the standard or specifications of that content. Taking time to create a table of contents or mock-up of a document

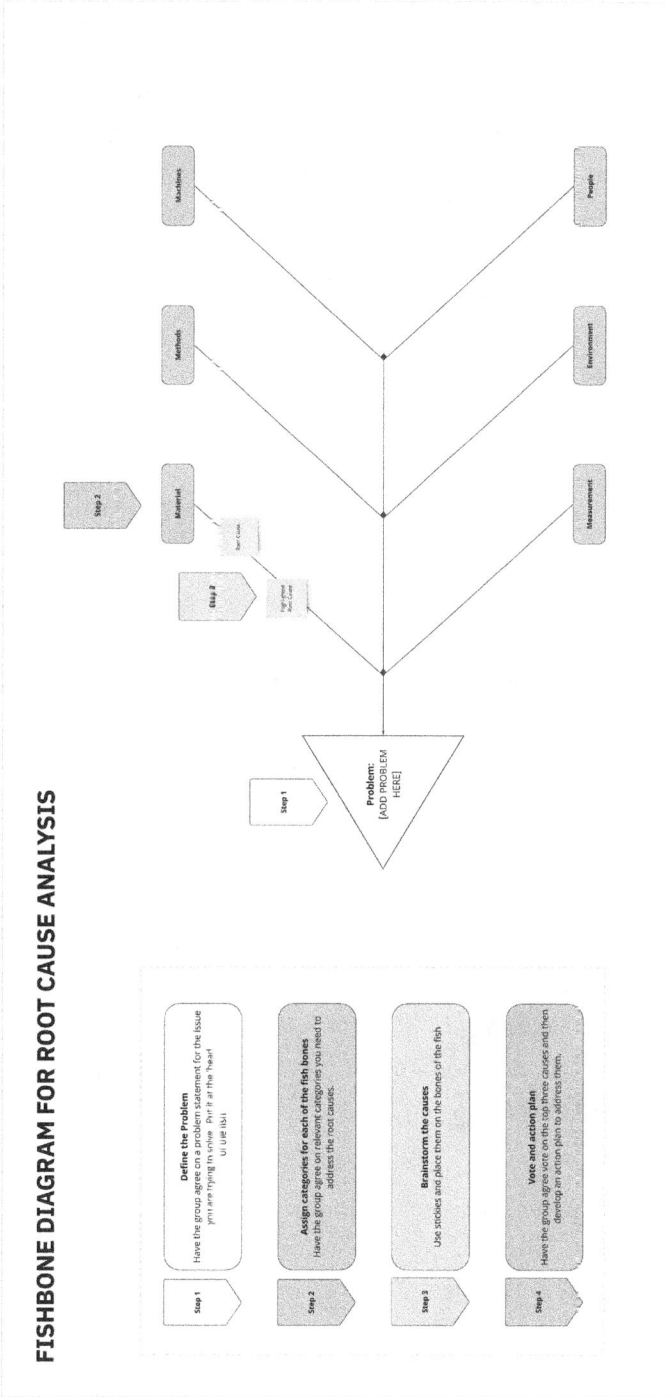

Figure 4.7 Fishbone diagram

or design element will go a long way to ensuring their understanding. Another strategy I've deployed frequently is to cocreate the content—working together on it can often get the customer focused and improve the quality of the content they create. Even if you start the cocreation process and send them away with homework, that can go a long way to having them understand your expectations.

In the second case, when decisions aren't turned around in a timely fashion, this points to a stakeholder that hasn't been engaged adequately or missed scope on the customer side. This allows you to revisit your RACI and an opportunity to onboard them appropriately. If this change is significant, for example, a whole department needs to be engaged, it will be critical to revisit your project success criteria and possibly recalculate your project PLOs and critical path.

Finally, I've found that one of the keys to negotiating changes is *yes but*—always say yes to sponsors and project customers but then discuss the implications. The key to having this discussion is referring to your project priority triangle and project success criteria. If you discuss the implications of the change, you can keep the conversation focused on facts and data instead of emotion or who yells the loudest.

If I were to "script" that conversation, it would go kind of like this.

Issue Inputs

> *Initiator*: We would like to add a new module to the application you are building.
>
> *Background*: We are launching a new product and need this module to be able to support our internal sales department

Options/Alternatives

1. Build/install the new module.
2. Have the internal sales department manually do the work needed.
3. Have the internal sales department utilize existing software to work around and support them.

> *Deliver*: The project team recommends the internal sales department to utilize existing software (notes, spreadsheets, and shared docs) to support the new product and that this functionality be built in a

future release/iteration. This is recommended because our priority for this project is time, and it will be several months before the volume of sales of this product warrants the time and effort required to customize the application.

What Do We Need From Whom?: The project team needs the project sponsor and project customer to agree with this recommendation as well as support the future iteration of the application and obtain appropriate funding and resources.

3P Agenda for Our Meeting With the Project Sponsor
and Customer

Purpose: To decide whether to change project priorities for a change request related to the introduction of product C.

Process:
- Review the initiator's request and the project team's recommendation.
- Discussion, Q&A.
- Decision (see 3.5 Making Decisions for tools).
- Project sponsor and customer support the recommendation from the project team and communicate to the initiator and the department *or* the project sponsor and customer adjust the project priorities, budget, and success criteria to include the new scope.

Payoff: Expectations of the project sponsor and customer are aligned and communicated to the project team.

Now, that wasn't such a bad conversation, was it?

3.5 Making Decisions

One of the most common complaints I hear in projects is "Why won't someone make a decision!?!" It can be within the project team, but it's usually pointed at the executive in the organization. It's also a real problem for project teams, particularly those that have projects with a focus on time or a tight deadline. Slow or no decision can dramatically affect our project deadlines as well as impact team morale.

What can get even more complicated are our projects that are to be delivered to external customers—because we don't have one organization to deal with, it's bound to be more complicated.

What I've found over the years is that this is a symptom of our old hierarchical organization structures and the tension or friction with dynamic teams and other factors such as:

- Folks with specialized knowledge aren't always the best at expressing themselves; they can struggle to communicate succinctly without jargon.
- It's not clear who in the organization has the authority to make decisions; there can often be a formal structure and an informal structure or reality.
- Organizations can be paralyzed by trying to make perfect decisions and are so risk-averse that they effectively decide to do nothing at all.
- Decision makers don't understand the implications of their decisions or conversely don't understand the implications of not deciding.

In the case of our internal organization working with an external customer, all the foregoing is true and can be exacerbated by a lack of clarity on who can decide while saving face in both organizations.

If any of that rings true in your organization or project, I can't change that situation; however, I can recommend a set of collaborative decision techniques that you can try out when your project gets stuck and you need a decision made.

The beauty of these techniques is that they don't require tons of analysis, but they do have some key elements. They are based on the principles of:

- Harnessing the knowledge of the group
- Encouraging contributions from everyone
- Making the right decision for right now, not the perfect decision for all time
- Using collaboration to support our project culture of freedom and responsibility

A collaborative decision meeting will follow a standard format and allow you to have some variation based on the type of decision you're making. Here's a templated agenda.

Purpose: Why are we having this meeting? To make a decision.
Process: What is the process we are going to use to arrive at the payoff?
1. Framing
2. Evaluating alternatives
3. Voting
4. Communicating results and next steps
Payoff: A decision is made, and a communication plan is established.

Let's cover each part of the process to better understand the different methods involved as well as some alternative approaches and considerations when selecting them.

Getting the Right People in the Room

We've spent time in previous chapters about roles and responsibilities—refer to 1.1 Frame the Problem, 1.2 Contextualize, and 2.2 People & Timeline, and don't forget our more recent discussions in 3.1 Build Team & Calendar. Just in case you've not read all those sections, let's summarize or consolidate that material into a few key points to ensure you get the right people in the room for the meeting!

- If the decision relates to the timeline, scope, or budget, the project sponsor and customer *must* be invited. Then it's specific to your organization on who overrules who; that is typically based on organization structure and titles.
- When the decision involves scope, you need to ensure that the appropriate resources are in the room to frame, discuss the alternatives, and articulate the next steps and their impacts. This means getting as close as possible to the process owners and subject matter experts to leverage their knowledge.
- For this meeting, I highly recommend that the project manager works with a facilitator to conduct the meeting. This allows one

person to be neutral throughout as well as allows the PM to provide input and do some active listening during the discussion.

Framing

We have discussed a variety of ways to frame conversations throughout the book. You'll perhaps remember the techniques we learned in the Listen chapter, utilizing problem statements, customer journey maps, and OKRs. Also, we used success criteria in the Understand chapter. All or a combination of these can be used, just making sure that you don't belabor the framing—make it succinct and audience appropriate.

"Audience appropriate" is dictated by the level in the organization of the attendees as well as the attendees' intimacy with the project itself. If they have not been actively and intensely involved, it may be appropriate to have a premeeting with the audience member to brief them and answer questions before the actual decision meeting. It's important to have everyone on an even playing field and agree on definitions before evaluating alternatives.

Evaluating Alternatives

Now that we have framed the decision and gotten everyone on the same page, we need to use collaborative methods to evaluate the alternatives and I have three approaches that I recommend. Table 4.4 has some considerations for when to use them.

Let's go through each of these in more detail.

Brainstorming Pros and Cons

This brainstorming is about the pros and cons of each alternative and is intended to gather input from everyone in the meeting. Also, remember that you don't want to have more than two alternatives—if you do have more than that you aren't deciding, you are exploring possibilities—that's a different meeting!!

This brainstorming is best suited for groups that are familiar with the decision, particularly the context and the situation. It will achieve rapid

Table 4.4 Evaluating alternative tools

Approach	Format	Consideration
Brainstorming pros and cons	If you have two choices: Do x or y	This works best for situations where the framing of the problem is well understood by the group; it's at enough level of detail for the group to understand the implications of each alternative
Weighted scoping	Multiple criteria that have different "value" to the decision overall	This works well particularly with mathematical folks but may drive some of the right-brained folks a little batty. It's a great way to bring quantification to a decision and remove or at least curtail the emotion involved in a decision. I find this effective with groups that have stakeholders with very different objectives, that is, Sales versus Product Development. It puts focus on the facts, not the power dynamics of the two groups
PICK charts	Weighing complex alternatives	If you have alternatives that are complex and a wide variety of opinions, this can bring a common language to the discussion of the alternatives. Also, it brings focus to the corporate benefit of each alternative

results (less time in your meeting) and should focus on ensuring that everyone is heard in preparation for voting.

Each person writes as many ideas as possible in the prescribed time for each alternative, both positive and negative—silent brainstorming. Then you have each person present their list of pros and cons or allow the group time to read the material and answer questions. Then we vote! It can also be appropriate, when the decision is long ranging—affecting strategic direction, for example—to then repeat. Have each person explain why they voted the way they did and then vote again.

Figure 4.8 shows the template for this type of decision.

This template is also available in PDF at www.pmgameboard.com/product/delphi-decision-template/.

Weighted Scoring

This is a practice I learned years ago when evaluating procurement decisions, particularly responses to RFPs or RFQs. It's a great way to boil a lot of information down to some quantifiable metrics. At the end of the exercise, the scores you create still need to resonate with the group's gut feeling. This method works particularly well when we are evaluating alternatives relative to project success criteria.

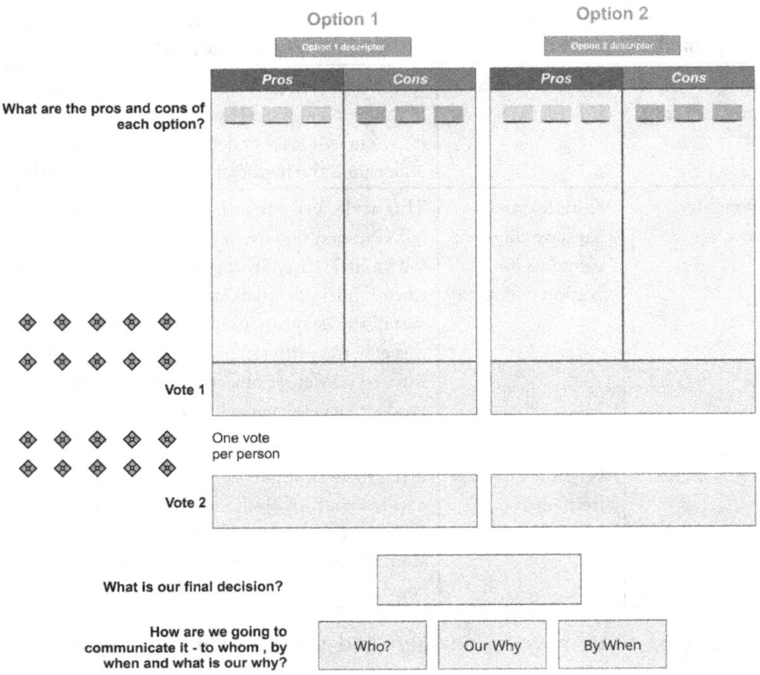

Figure 4.8 Delphi decision model template

For this portion of the meeting, you would prepare a grid for each success criterion and each alternative (again if you have more than three alternatives, you aren't in a decision-making meeting, you are developing alternatives!) and have the group agree on the weight of each success criteria—high or medium (you can't have low or it isn't a success criterion)—and then determine for each alternative what the score is relative to each success criteria: Does it meet, exceed or is the requirement not met? You'll end up with a grid that looks like Figure 4.9.

Then you can translate them into scores; for the weight I use 10 and medium use 5. Then meet = 1, exceeded = 2, and not met = 0. Your table will then look like Figure 4.10.

So, at the end of this evaluation, you know that alternative 1 is the top one, closely followed by alternative 3 and distantly alternative 2. You'll want the group to reconfirm that these numbers reflect what they are seeing or feeling in their gut; otherwise, circle back and resolve any discrepancies in either the weighting or the score. Don't discourage these types

Weighted Scoring Matrix	Weight	Alternative 1 Score	Alternative 2	Alternative 3
Criterion 1	High	Meet	Not met	Meet
Criterion 2	High	Exceed	Meet	Exceed
Criterion 3	Medium	Not met	Exceed	Meet
Criterion 4	Medium	Exceed	Meet	Not met
Criterion 5	High	Meet	Not met	Meet

Figure 4.9 Weighted scoring

Weighted Scoring Matrix	Weight	Alternative 1 Score	Alternative 2	Alternative 3
Criterion 1	10	1	0	1
Criterion 2	10	2	1	2
Criterion 3	5	0	2	1
Criterion 4	5	2	1	0
Criterion 5	10	1	0	1
		50	25	45

Figure 4.10 Weighted scoring with numbers

of discussions as they provide invaluable information on stakeholder expectations.

PICK Charts

We first discussed the PICK chart in the Listen chapter, when we were evaluating our project idea. But let's explore it from the technique perspective so you can apply it in any situation.

PICK chart stands for possible, implement, challenge, and kill. It is a great tool to use in situations when trying to decide on multiple complex alternatives. I've used it for years in the situations of:

- At the Listen stage of a project in two circumstances:
  - To clarify different strategies to achieve the success criteria for a project.
  - To evaluate multiple projects and decide which ones to give priority and resources.

- At the Understand leg of a project to evaluate different key components against the project success criteria; more to come on that in the Understand chapter.
- During the Create leg of the project, evaluate potential solutions to a problem encountered at this stage of the project.

Purpose of This Tool

The PICK tool is used to simplify decision making and compare alternatives. This visual tool allows you to solicit input from multiple stakeholders and present the information clearly. It is a scatter plot with two axes:

- Vertical axis = the benefit to the organization.
- Horizontal axis = the effort required.
- Each axis is scaled from low to high.
- There are four quadrants in the chart:
  o *P*ossible.
  o *I*mplement. (Just do it.)
  o *C*hallenge.
  o *K*ill.

How to Use the PICK Tool

1. Set the context of the choices to be made.
2. Discuss the different alternatives and ensure that everyone understands and is aligned in a general fashion with the scope of each idea and project.
3. Take good notes to use in future project discussions.
4. Have the group rank each alternative project in terms of benefit and effort.

I find that cards in Miro work particularly well for this type of meeting. See Figure 4.11. They allow you to populate more information into each alternative along with people assigned and due dates.

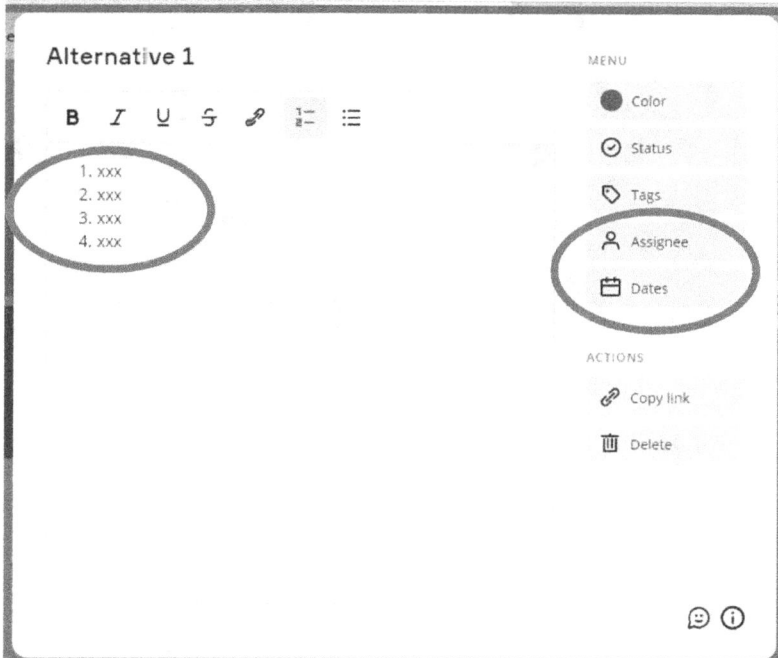

Figure 4.11 Miro cards

Don't forget you'll have to build these cards before the meeting—these are known alternatives. You may update some of these alternatives during the meeting as clarification for your next steps and communication. So, you'll end up with a space on a board that looks like Figure 4.12.

Deciding

We've now framed the decision and evaluated the alternatives so it's time to decide. When doing this in a meeting, I find the most direct way to do this visually is to either dot vote or vote anonymously. Frankly, I've found that anonymous voting is cumbersome and takes more time than makes sense. However, you may find that for some contentious decisions, this is the preferred method, but I'm afraid if that's truly a requirement, you don't have a psychologically safe environment and probably have other

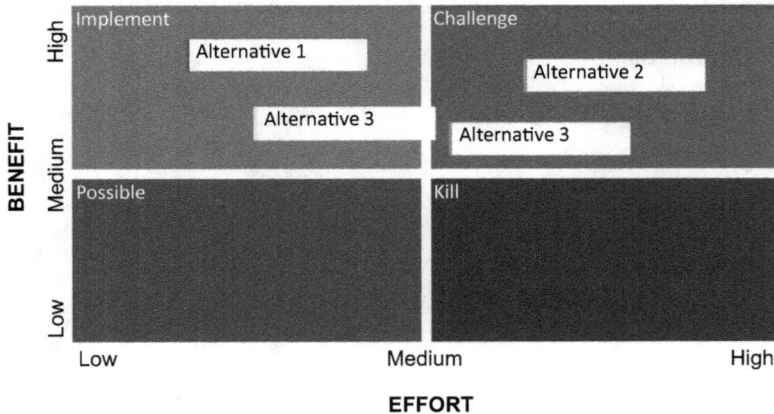

Figure 4.12 PICK alternatives

issues to work on. Dot voting is straightforward; have one dot per participant and then select their preferred alternative.

Then once complete, you can summarize the results and get agreement on whether the group is ready to move on to communicating the decision. In some cases, it may be appropriate to have each participant present why they voted the way they did and then revote. I've found this works well when you have larger groups and there is a split vote, for example, 4–3 and 5–4.

Communicating the Decision and Next Steps

This is all about determining who does what, by when, and where people can provide comments, questions, and feedback. Also, don't forget that the next steps will often be executed by folks other than the decision makers in the room; so the who does what by when may consist of communication back to the project team for them to detail the next steps.

Key Decisions

Projects require a myriad of decisions, but there are some key project decisions that I want to highlight (Table 4.5). Refer to that chapter/section for details on completing those workshops.

So, we've now got no excuses for your project team not being able to make a decision. Remember, it's not about making the perfect decision

Table 4.5 Key project decisions

PMGB Leg and Step	Decision	Recommended Method
Listen—1.5 Viable Idea	Based on all the information gathered in the Listen leg, is this a viable idea?	Pros and cons
Listen—Go/No Go	Based on the information gathered and relative to all the initiatives underway and our resourcing, is this a good time to proceed with this project?	PICK chart
Understand—2.2 People & Timeline	Evaluating the resources or solution proposed in the procurement process	Weighted scoring matrix
Understand—Go/No Go	Based on the planning completed in this leg, is this project still going to deliver the benefits identified in the Listen leg and is this the appropriate time to proceed?	Pros and cons
Create—3.4 Manage Changes	Does the change justify changing our project priorities?	Dot vote or PICK chart
Create—Go/No Go	Is the project complete?	Weighted scoring matrix

for all time; it's about making a decision that helps the project team move forward.

In summary, Figure 4.13 shows the techniques that you can mix and match for your decision meeting.

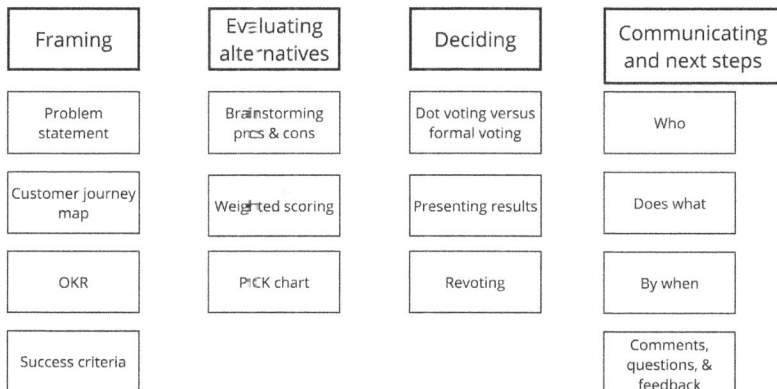

Framing	Evaluating alternatives	Deciding	Communicating and next steps
Problem statement	Brainstorming pros & cons	Dot voting versus formal voting	Who
Customer journey map	Weighted scoring	Presenting results	Does what
OKR	PICK chart	Revoting	By when
Success criteria			Comments, questions, & feedback

Figure 4.13 Decision flow

Create Go/No Go & Learn

Looks like we're sprinting to the finish line! Just a couple more steps until we begin to work on closing our project and the Reflect leg of the board! We've got a final Go/No Go and one more Learn to complete.

Go/No Go

This Go/No Go is all about ensuring we deliver what the customer wants. Ideally, this is as simple as meeting with the customer, reviewing the success criteria, and making the decision. However, if there is a lack of clarity around whether the project is complete, I recommend that project teams use a Must, Should, and Nice to Have list.

This is developed by mapping the critical deliverables you identified in the Understand leg—2.1 Scope of Work—into a list with the addition of those new deliverables identified in your weekly status meetings. This list is then categorized into Must, Should, and Nice to Have, reviewed with the customer, and agreed on the thresholds that need to be achieved to close the project.

The Must-Have will never be negotiable; they are there, or they aren't; some may be incomplete because there have been defects identified that need to be resolved, but they all need to be complete and accepted by the customer.

The negotiation comes with the Shoulds—are these adequately completed? The keys to this negotiation are:

- Defining adequately. For example, you may have said in the success criteria that what needs to be done was to have everyone trained; however, in your Must, Should, and Nice to Have, this may have been broken down into you Must have 100 percent of the core users trained and Should have 80 percent of the rest of the staff trained. Perhaps, there is a negotiable timeframe to complete the balance of the training. The trick here is to negotiate scope by setting a mutually agreeable threshold and getting a fixed date for when things will be completed.

- Defining complete. Again, this is all about defining what complete means. In our example about training, it is important that *all* the rest of the success criteria, Musts, and Shoulds are complete and then perhaps there is an agreement that only the training portion of the project and associate resources continues for a fixed period.
- In the case of a software project, do you typically have a "warranty period" where defects are resolved? There may be an opportunity to complete the scope in that period while continuing to close the project.
- Are there future phases of the project? These Shoulds could be moved forward to another phase, release, or future iteration.

Once these are all resolved, it's time to move on to the Learn part of this leg.

Learn

This Learn segment is particularly important because if there are ever going to be lessons learned, it will be in the Create leg. Teams and projects can sail through Listen and Understand, but the real pressure test is in this leg—delivering value, and responding to project changes, all while maintaining a great team culture!

In the Listen leg, our retrospective focused on improving project initiation practices; in our Understand leg, our retrospective focused on team norms and/or project planning. For this leg, we'll want to focus on the Create steps and be sure to revisit our team norms. We'll save the juicy, end-to-end retrospective for our Reflect leg.

For our team norms portion, we'll follow the same format as we did in Understand; however, there are a couple of key tweaks:

- The retrospective will be focused on passing on lessons learned to the next project or team as this one will soon be disbanded.
- It's important to use the five whys to get to the root cause in this retrospective; some things we experienced in this leg may reflect on the Listen or Understand practices we used.

- Our retrospective actions are delivered to the project sponsor and project customer; this will better ensure that these are carried forward to future projects. However, if your organization has a Project Management Office, this is also where they would be communicated to.

The 3P agenda for this retrospective would look like this.

Purpose: Why are we having this meeting? To reflect on how our team norms performed during the Create leg and cocreate lessons for next time.

Process: What is the process we are going to use to arrive at the payoff?
1. Icebreaker activity.
2. Review the team norms developed as part of your project kickoff.
3. Silent brainstorming about what worked well for each norm.
4. Have everyone group the ideas into common themes.
5. For each theme, develop a plan to reinforce or continue this success.
6. Silent brainstorming of what did not work for each norm.
7. Have everyone group the ideas into common themes.
8. Do some root cause analysis on why—use five whys to ensure you get beyond the symptoms.
9. Develop recommendations for the next project team to address these issues.
10. Determine the communication messages from this retrospective to be passed to the project sponsor and project customer.

Payoff: Ensuring that we continuously learn and improve our project team performance.

Next, for our retrospective on the practices in this leg, again we'll mimic what we did in the Understand leg; however, we'll tweak these to account for the fact that the team will probably be disbanding soon. The 3P agenda would like this.

Purpose: Why are we having this meeting? To ensure that our project delivery processes are working well.

Process: What is the process we are going to use to arrive at the payoff?

1. Icebreaker activity.
2. Review the key dates and activities completed in this leg:
   - o 3.1 Build Team and Calendar.
   - o 3.2 Enable Team.
   - o 3.3 Create Deliverables.
   - o 3.4 Manage Change.
   - o 3.5 Make Decisions.
3. Silent brainstorm what works well for project delivery overall.
4. Have everyone group the ideas into common themes.
5. For each theme, develop a plan to reinforce or continue this success.
6. Silent brainstorming of what did not work for each activity.
7. Have everyone group the ideas into common themes.
8. Do some root cause analysis on why—use five whys to ensure you get beyond the symptoms.
9. Develop recommendations for the next project team to address these issues.
10. Determine the communication messages from this retrospective to be passed to the project sponsor, project customer, and your PMO if applicable.

Payoff: Ensuring our project delivery is continuously improved.

Congrats! That's the heavy lifting done on this project; now we move on to Reflect, where we'll dot our i's and cross our t's and most importantly celebrate our success!

In Summary

We have covered a *lot* of territory in this chapter! I'm sure that no one will use all these techniques because, frankly, that's probably not appropriate to your unique project. What I do hope is that this has provided some insights into different techniques you can try when you're in this critical leg of your project delivering value but also ensuring you sustain and nurture a culture of freedom and responsibility in your project team!

If you:

- Take time to build the team and enable them to have great relationships and processes upfront
- Create clear accountabilities along with a shared understanding of those responsibilities
- Find creative and customized ways for your team to interact, communicate, and manage time scope, and budget
- Have processes in place to not just manage change but also manage expectations
- Get decisions made that build on consensus and get made

Then you'll do amazing things with your project and your team!

CHAPTER 5

Reflect—Learning and Celebrating

Overview

We are now moving away from project delivery and starting to wind down the project. At this stage, the project team will be disbanded and the project will transition to day-to-day operations. We'll also be off-boarding our vendors and/or closing contracts with suppliers.

In this chapter, we're going to highlight some of the key attributes of successful project reflection: off-boarding team members and vendors, lessons learned, customer sign-off, as well as a discussion about benefits realization after we've understood what comes next.

It's important to remember that this leg of a project is heavily focused on closing out project documentation: contracts, purchase orders, change requests, and so on. We aren't going to spend time on these topics as there are numerous resources available online; we're going to focus on wrapping up the project with an emphasis on continuous learning—in projects and the organization overall.

For this leg (see Figure 5.1), we have:

- 4.1 What's Next: Is there a next phase of this project? Are we handing the project off internally or to a client? How do we set the next project and team up for success?
- 4.2 Retrospectives: How do we reflect on team culture, really learn, and even recover from a project?
- 4.3 Off-Board Our Vendors: These folks have been an integral part of our project delivery and we want to gather feedback from them specifically focused on improving our procurement processes. We also want to give them feedback, positive and negative, particularly in cases where these vendors are important to future projects.

4. REFLECT

Project Closure

4.1 What's Next?

4.2 Retrospectives

4.3 Off-Board Vendors

4.4 Off-Board People

4.5 Celebrate Success

Customer Sign-Off!

That's a wrap!

Figure 5.1 Reflect

- 4.4 Off-Board Our People: Project team members make a big commitment to our project often while continuing their operational role and we want to recognize their efforts and ensure they get feedback to enhance their next project experience and/or their career.
- 4.5 Celebrate Success: This is in addition to the small and timely celebrations we've had along the way and must include not only the project team but also the sponsor, customer, and other key stakeholders.
- Customer Sign-Off: Dotting the i's and crossing the t's with the customer; everything from closing the loop on OKRs to handing over to the operations team in the case of systems projects or to the business department for process improvement projects.

4.1 What's Next?

A key part of closing off our project is understanding what's next—numerous projects don't end—it is a closing of this phase, iteration, release, or version that will start after this project is completed. Therefore, closing a project versus closing a phase is quite different. For a straightforward project closing checklist, check out www.teamwork.com/blog/project-closure/.

If you are closing your project, then skip to 4.2 Retrospectives. If your project has a follow-on phase or iteration, then you'll want to set up a new phase and a new team for success. We'll cover the key assets from this project to pass along to the next phase.

Setting Up a New Phase for Success

If our project has future phases, there are some key elements we want to ensure that inform the next phase. Key items are:

- The lessons learned or retrospectives from each leg of the project. In particular, those from the Listen leg will help them get started on the right foot. I've found that if we did a good job of the Listen leg in this phase particularly with 1.1 Framing the Problem and 1.2 Contextualizing, then these may be reusable and accelerate the team's ability to complete initiating the next phase.
- The Resource Strategy in 1.4 can offer insights into the next phase, particularly about resources acquired outside the organization. If vendors were used in this phase, our project can be a great source of information—both positive and negative on who to use, their responsiveness, fit with the team, and ability to deliver.
- The material from the Listen leg of our project can be helpful to onboard new stakeholders for a future phase and to complete the project kickoff.
- The scope items we gathered as part of Create and specifically 3.3 Create Deliverables and our Must, Should, and Nice to Have list that was finalized as part of Go/No Go at the end of the leg will potentially provide scope for the next phase. The same would be true for any change requests that we decided not to proceed with in 3.4 Manage Change.

Setting Up a New Project Team for Success

We had some great team support in our project—everything from the team norms we established early in the project, to the communication strategies we utilized as well as the feedback gathered along the way about team performance concerning norms. We'll want to share that information with the next project team.

With the next phase of the project, look for opportunities to resource the team differently—providing learning opportunities for different people as well as mentoring from existing team members in the next phase.

If the project team will see a lot of new members or a significant change in the outsourced portion of the resourcing or even potentially a new vendor involved, then I would recommend utilizing the opportunity to step back and see what best served the team in terms of establishing norms and communication. Refer to the lessons learned on team culture in 4.2 Retrospectives, coming up next.

Also, be cognizant of where the broader organization is relative to culture and values. The best companies that are values based will refresh this material regularly and you want your project team to align with the most current thinking in the organization and not stray into the wilderness.

4.2 Retrospectives

From a PMGB perspective, there are some key ways to do retrospectives that reinforce continuous improvement and a project culture of freedom and responsibility. Do them often; do them thoughtfully—get to the root cause but also don't forget to mix them up.

The Basics

I've found that every lesson learned or retrospective benefits from providing context to the exercise in a couple of areas:

- Having rules of engagement for the workshop, things like:
  o No bad ideas.
  o No finger-pointing.
  o One conversation at a time.

- Icebreakers to get the creative juices flowing:
  o Fresh thinking.
  o Creative problem solving.
  o Mix them up—don't let them get stale!
- An overview of the project stage we are reflecting on to frame the discussion:
  o What was the problem we were trying to solve with the project?
  o Who has been involved?
  o Key milestones.
  o Key results for this project or this phase.

This can level-set the team and help them to put the exercise in context and not just focus on what has happened most recently.

If project teams apply lessons learned or retrospectives at each stage of the project, then they are building on their knowledge at each phase and are adopting a learning environment in their project. Also, retrospectives can be utilized when project teams hit a snag in a project—to ensure they reflect and apply those lessons right away. I recommend that, *at a minimum*, project teams do a retrospective at the end of each phase; Listen, Understand, and Create.

For some general information on retrospectives, check out www.atlassian.com/team-playbook/plays/retrospective. Also, Miro has a plethora of templates on retrospectives in the Miroverse, so check them out (www.miro.com/miroverse/retrospectives/). Make sure to mix them up and don't use the same old format every time; you want to get the creative juices flowing in these sessions!

Again, these can be started with whatever your favorite format is—what worked well and what didn't, mad, sad, glad, and longed for, and so on. Then go deeper by using tools such as the five whys or the fishbone diagram to understand the root cause of the issue. This is really where the learning is developed.

Next, I'll go into more detail about:

- Retrospectives with customers.
- Doing lessons learned on team culture: How do we get deeper than "we had such a great team"?

- Lessons learned as therapy: This is a particular approach to use when a project goes off the rails and there is animosity between project team members. This is important if they are going to have to work together on a future project or simply as a catharsis for the benefit of everyone's mental health!

Retrospectives With Customers

Customers are incredibly valuable and rich sources of feedback on our projects. They can provide unique insights about the true impact of our project and there may be multiple layers of customers. Don't forget that while there is a customer for the project, that customer has customers as well (or in the case of sales or marketing, potential customers). Remember too that internal departments are customers. The Research and Development department or back-office groups such as Accounting also have customers! I encourage project teams to look for the broadest definition of customer possible to gather feedback. You'll want to think through these various levels of customers to determine the strategy to solicit their input.

This is best illustrated by an example. Think of a situation where you are deploying software to a particular department to improve their interactions with their customers. For example, the sales department is deploying a new Customer Relationship Management (CRM) system, which will better support their interactions with potential customers as well as existing customers. Our project to deploy that software could solicit input from customers and prospects on how well that deployment went as well as our internal customers—the sales folks themselves. It could also include internal departments that are customers of the CRM information—everyone from senior executives who receive reports on sales performance to accounting who use the information to calculate commissions, even the warranty department which uses sales data to project workload.

I have a couple of rules of thumb when considering soliciting this input:

- Go as broad as possible to solicit input from customers; don't just look at people that the project had direct contact with but also look at those that have intermittent contact with either the project team or the deliverables.

- Spend effort soliciting feedback or input that is commensurate with the cost of the project. If you were implementing a new CRM, this would probably be a $250k project in a small- to medium-sized organization (when you include the internal resource costs). That would mean you'd want to spend $1,000s on getting feedback or input, not $10,000s getting it.
- Solicit input by multiple methods that are reflective of their stake in the project. For high-value customers of the project, use retrospectives or focus groups and for lower-value customers, use surveys or polls.

Regardless of the methods you use, go as broadly as possible to solicit input and as deeply as their role in the project warrants.

The key to making this successful with customers is to appropriately frame the conversation—in this case, things like before and after, cycle times to perform key customer requests, the ease of use, look and feel, and the ability to get help when needed are all good ideas to help frame customer retrospectives.

Retrospectives on Team Culture

These are a very specialized form of retrospective, but they go to the core of the PMGB. These are also our early warning systems on issues in the team. If a project manager (PM) can use these diligently to monitor results over time, they can get ahead of potential issues or conflicts in the team.

We start building our team culture in our project kickoff meeting(s) and through these retrospectives, we continue to build and sustain it. We're all familiar with:

forming, storming, norming, and performing

(www.hr.mit.edu/learning-topics/teams/articles/stages-development) and these retrospectives will ensure that we get to norming and performing quickly and retain that culture in our project. So, in this section, we're going to go a little deeper and explore some techniques you might want to try out. Overall, the process we're going to use is given in Figure 5.2.

Monitoring Project Culture

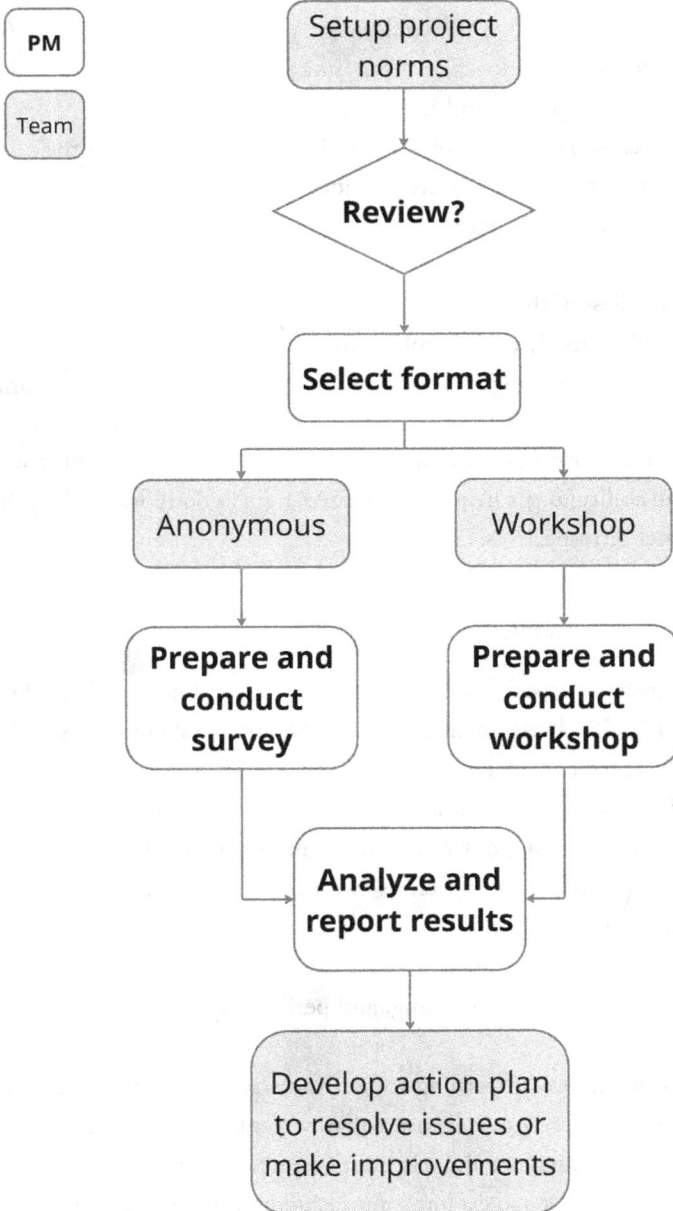

Figure 5.2 Monitoring project culture

This approach is based on some key steps and decisions and is supported by some of the tools that we've already described: brainstorming, grouping, five whys, and PICK charts. The process and the tools or techniques provide us with a way to get feedback on how our team is performing relative to our norms and to ensure we sustain or improve that performance. If we create team norms and then leave them on the shelf, it is unlikely we'll continue to have a great project culture or be able to handle the stressors that occur during a project and be able to respond to them.

Any system needs feedback to ensure its performance is optimized. I remember taking a process improvement course *many* moons ago from a fellow who consulted to McDonald's and helped them improve their processes. What is the one thing you can count on at McDonald's regardless of the location or even country that it's in—consistency? One of the systems they optimized early on to ensure that customers received what they ordered was a feedback system; that's why all the drive-throughs have screens for you to check your order.

Also, there is the principle that if you can't measure it, you can't manage it. Measurement gives you feedback not only on the current state but also on the trend over time. This is particularly important when it comes to project culture! As we move our teams through forming, norming, storming, and performing, we want to sustain the performing piece as we move on to the Create leg of the project where things will get intense!

Let's go through each of the steps and briefly review what's happening:

- Set up project norms: Remember you did this at project kickoff—in the Understand leg or the Create leg.
- Review: As PM, you may have different triggers to initiate or know that it's time for a review. Considerations are:
  - You want to make sure you check in regularly with the team as trending over time, getting feedback, and even the act of measuring itself, ensures that your project team's culture is an area of focus. This also helps stress the importance of our project culture to the team.
  - You can use these retrospectives to nip a situation in the bud; when there is tension in the team, interpersonal

challenges, team members are not engaged, or any type of conflict, this can be an intervention to resolve issues and repair project culture.

    o At least, at the end of each leg, check in with the team before the next leg.

- Select format: This is the decision to have either a workshop format or an anonymous asynchronous format. This will be dependent on the dynamics of the team at that point in time and can be used to ensure anonymity and help ensure that team members will participate more openly. Check out the considerations in Table 5.1.

- Conduct a survey or workshop. This is where you'll gather the feedback. Again, see Table 5.1 for some considerations. Also, a couple of tips about surveys:

    o Be sure to use at least a 7-point scale. You want to be able to clearly delineate the extremes and neutral.

    o Ask for quantitative scores so you can track trends over time; however, also allow for open-ended or free-format feedback. Having the team provide an example of a situation can be enormously helpful when developing the root cause of why things have broken down in the team.

- Develop an action plan to resolve this. Whether you've done a survey or a team workshop, you'll want the team to develop the root cause of the issues and, in particular, the action plan to resolve them. This will ensure that the team provides insights into the root causes and that the team takes accountability for the action plan.

There is a template in the Miroverse for this workshop at www.miro.com/miroverse/team-pulse-check-template/. Also, see Figure 5.3. There is also a PDF version at www.pmgameboard.com/product/project-team-norm-feedback-template/.

Some considerations when deciding which techniques to use for these retrospectives are given in Table 5.1.

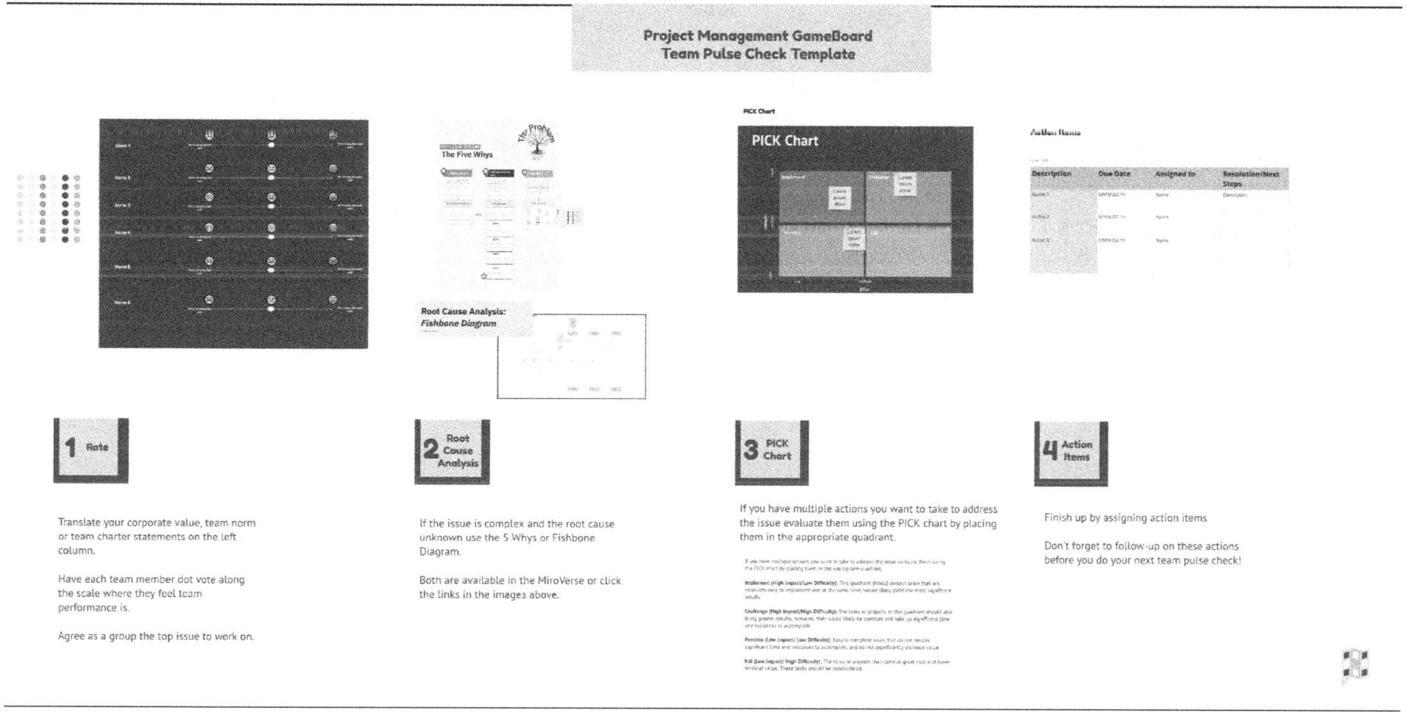

Project Management GameBoard
Team Pulse Check Template

1 Rate

Translate your corporate value, team norm or team charter statements on the left column.

Have each team member dot vote along the scale where they feel team performance is.

Agree as a group the top issue to work on.

2 Root Cause Analysis

Root Cause Analysis:
Fishbone Diagram

If the issue is complex and the root cause unknown use the 5 Whys or Fishbone Diagram.

Both are available in the MiroVerse or click the links in the image 3 above.

3 PICK Chart

PICK Chart

If you have multiple actions you want to take to address the issue evaluate them using the PICK chart by placing them in the appropriate quadrant.

4 Action Items

Author Name

Finish up by assigning action items

Don't forget to follow-up on these actions before you do your next team pulse check!

Figure 5.3 Team feedback template

Table 5.1 Retrospective techniques

Situation	Format	Templates and Tools
New team	Anonymous feedback as the group may be uncomfortable vocalizing issues or questions with each other	Survey on team norms with a 7- to 10-point scale
Periodic check-in	Have each person rate each of the team norms about how they feel the team is performing. Take the one to two lowest performers, do a root cause analysis, and develop an action plan	Sentiment analysis, brainstorm space, five whys, PICK chart
Team that is tense, stressed, or in conflict	Anonymous feedback with comments to obtain the most honest feedback and information possible. Consider utilizing a facilitator for a workshop on root causes and action plan development	Brainstorm space, five whys, PICK chart
Trends over time	Surveys with a scaled score	Box and Whisker to determine min and max and monitor trends
Friction with customer or sponsor	Review team norms with the project team to determine where there are issues and brainstorm the root causes of the issues. Review the issues with the customer and sponsor to get feedback and determine if they can resolve them or if the entire group needs to meet to agree on root causes and next steps	Brainstorm space, five whys, PICK chart

Team Culture Trends

One thing to pay attention to when you are measuring team culture and gathering your pulse checks is to keep track of the results over time. The PM must be aware of how things are trending. I would recommend that every check-in is tracked with not only the results but a commentary on the status of the project overall, along with a regular cadence to step back and review the results.

Retrospectives as Therapy

I mentioned earlier the lessons learned when a project (or a phase) hasn't gone well and has resulted in bad feelings between project members and perhaps even between departments. In this case, the exercise can be treated as more of a cathartic exercise to repair relationships, wipe the slate clean, and learn from mistakes made.

For this situation, it's often best to have a third-party facilitator do the workshop. Having someone who is recognized as neutral can be hugely beneficial to get to the root of the issues and be truly constructive on actions and the next steps.

This type of retrospective is particularly important if there is a next phase to the project or where relationships have been damaged between departments that need to work together going forward.

4.3 Off-Board Our Vendors

This is often neglected in project teams or in managing supplier relationships, but in our collaborative world, we want to encourage this! Usually, at the end of a project, the PM or the procurement department will give suppliers a scorecard or, in the worst cases, end up in lawsuits for deficiencies—this is not the way to build these relationships and improve them. To get the most out of our vendor–supplier relationships and our project teams, we need to build and continually improve these relationships. The two keys are to gather feedback and then understand the implications for the next project, so we'll cover those in more detail.

Gathering Supplier Feedback

We want to improve two things in particular—our relationship with our suppliers as well as our procurement practices. To gather this input effectively, you'll want to start with the resourcing strategy that was developed in the Listen leg—1.4, add the work done in the Understand leg, particularly around 2.1 Scope of Work, 2.2 People & Timeline, and 2.3 Budget & Equipment. It also wouldn't hurt to include the information from 2.4 Quality & Risk in relation specifically to quality as well as communication.

Once you've gathered all this material, this can help frame a discussion with suppliers—what worked well and what didn't. Again, as we did with other retrospectives, make the effort you spend on this exercise commensurate with the project budget as well as the proportion of that budget spent on vendors. So, if we take our CRM example of the $250k project, there will have been a significant portion of that money spent with the vendor/supplier. That means we'll want to spend the time doing a thorough retrospective with the supplier. It might also be beneficial to include the procurement folks in this same activity.

Having a retrospective with suppliers is a unique undertaking; it requires a special type of trust between two organizations and, to be effective, needs to be tightly scripted. I find this is true because of several factors:

- Some project organizations have immature procurement practices and are contracting with sophisticated vendors. This can lead to situations where vendor relationships are consistently mismanaged and ineffective. This maturity is never improved because each project that experiences problems is perceived as a one-off.
- Some project organizations manage their vendors by moving risk to the vendor with punitive contract terms and conditions. This is often the case with large organizations and small vendors. Under these circumstances, vendors have complex inflexible contracts and vendors may not have the opportunity to deliver as much value as they could.
- Due to the nature of the customer and vendor relationship, there may be tension or mistrust that is hard to overcome to truly get actionable input. If the two organizations have very different cultures, this can also be a challenge. Therefore, if the retrospective is robustly scripted, you may get the best results possible without anyone fearing repercussions.

Now, let's look at what that retrospective agenda could look like.

Purpose: Why are we having this meeting? Cocreate a retrospective with our key supplier about our procurement and fulfillment in the project.

Process: What is the process we are going to use to arrive at the payoff?

- Review the project inputs:
  - Listen 1.4 Resource Strategy.
  - Understand inputs.
  - Create inputs.
- What worked well?
- What needs to improve?
- Action items and owners.

Payoff: We are continuously improving our project resourcing strategies, procurement practices, and best utilizing our vendors.

If you were facilitating this session in Miro, you could prepare a board that looks something like in Figure 5.4.

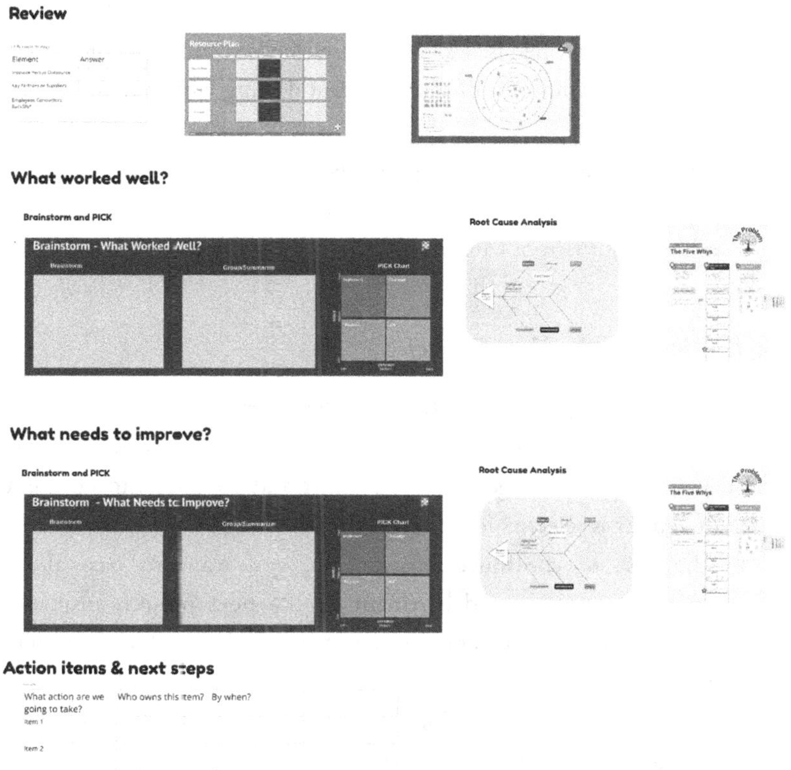

Review

What worked well?

What needs to improve?

Action items & next steps

Figure 5.4 Procurement retrospective

In the meeting, you'd also want to do a quick summary or refresher on the project timeline, particularly focusing on key vendor dates such as RFP, contract award, resources on site, and resources complete.

You'll notice that I've added the PICK chart as well as the fishbone diagram and the five whys. You probably won't use all these tools, but each of them adds value to the discussion in different ways:

- PICK chart. This helps ensure that the action items we identify truly add value. Also, because we are discussing corporate procurement practices, there may be some significant challenges, stakeholders, and systems to effect change. So, while it's important to identify these areas for improvement, it may take multiple projects experiencing the same problem before there is the corporate will to make changes.
- Fishbone. This is a great way to ensure that we look at all aspects of identified issues. We want to make sure that we aren't examining symptoms of problems but dealing with the root causes.
- Five whys. We covered this previously but again this is a great tool to get beyond the symptoms and ensure we are addressing the root cause.

Implications for the Next Project

As a result of doing a retrospective with your vendor(s), there are two likely outcomes: You had a positive experience with this vendor and would work with them again, or you didn't and you want to ensure a different vendor is selected for the next project.

In the case of continued relationship, you want to pass along either to the procurement department or the next project, probably through the sponsor or project customer as well as the vendor, the results of your review.

In the case of different vendors going forward, you'll want to ensure that procurement, the project sponsor, and the project customer understand the reasons why. It will also be critical for the next project to allow the time necessary to research (do a market scan) and procure a new vendor.

4.4 Off-Board Our Team

One of the keys to success in developing people in the organization is giving them the ability to develop through project work. Because so many organizations do not have dedicated teams assigned to projects and are often juggling multiple projects at the same time as day-to-day operations, projects are a great way to develop people—they can develop new skills in a supportive team.

Now this also assumes that when you resourced your project and particularly when you onboarded people to the project team the expectations for each resource were spelled out. Also, during the Create leg or execution phase of the project, you would have been monitoring individual and team performance and giving timely feedback to the project team, identifying the root cause of any issues and addressing them promptly.

So, this step is about giving people feedback on their project performance overall—this is like an individual retrospective and allows the PM to focus on each individual. This can improve not only the PM's performance but also the employee's performance on the next project; it is a particularly good time to recognize growth or skills that have been developed through the project.

Using the retrospective format reinforces the learning environment we want to encourage in project teams. Pick your favorite retrospective format—what went well, what didn't, what made you sad, glad, and what you longed for—just about any of them will do and have the project team member complete their thoughts before the meeting. Then get together and discuss them, focus on giving them constructive feedback and developing improvement plans or input into their personal developmental goals.

4.5 Celebrating Success

We want to spend a few minutes talking about celebrating success. Celebrating success after the project is a great way to recognize the effort expended, leaving everyone on a high from the project, and recognize the efforts of individual team members.

I've seen when this goes well and when it goes badly! The characteristics of a great celebration of a truly successful project are:

- Everyone agrees the project was a success, That is not just the view of the project team itself or a couple of interested executives, but the organization can collectively point to the project as a success and has a clear way to articulate why it was successful. Clear means measurable and strategically aligned.
- The celebration of success extends beyond a core group of people. I've seen people left out of celebrations—sometimes maliciously and sometimes just oversight. A true celebration recognized all the efforts—part-time and full-time participants, contractors, and suppliers as well as employees.
- The project team can shine in front of leaders and supervisors. Let's face it: People love opportunities for them to increase their personal brand and be recognized for their contributions.
- It's not about the amount of money spent—it's about the fun! I've had some of the best project celebrations involve ice cream cake and dollar store gifts to team members about their special contributions. Whether that was their sense of humor, how they handled a tricky project issue, or best attendance, those tried-and-true folks are always there to help. Get creative and use your imagination!

Hazards to watch out for with celebrating success:

- Err on the side of inclusion. For a large project that crosses organizational boundaries, don't get petty and leave one department out; this can affect organizational morale and, trust me, when you go to get project resources from that department next time, you'll probably struggle.

- Be careful, your celebration is commensurate with practices in the rest of the organization! No one wants to see project X have a huge celebration while project Y can't get the basic funding or resources they need to survive!

Customer Sign-Off

Our very last step on the PMGB is Customer Sign-Off. This helps reinforce one of our key principles: We start with the customer; we manage expectations with the customer throughout the project; and we end with the customer!

At this point, we are winding up the last key elements of this relationship to ensure that the customer can be successful going forward. These are:

- All your transition to operations activities. The customers' operational staff should be clear on their roles and responsibilities and fully trained to be able to perform the operational tasks required. It's not unusual to have a "warranty" period where project experts can be accessed, should issues arise. Be sure to negotiate with the customer what this agreement looks like and a fixed duration.
- Closing the loop with OKRs. Remember in Listen 1.2 Contextualize, we linked our project to organizational or strategic objectives and key results. We want to make sure that there are systems and processes in place to measure the results of our project. This will ensure that the investment in the project is realized. Also, it's important to pass these on to the project customer for future reporting.
- Closing the loop on our customer journey maps. As part of completing the project, the project customer may need to update SOPs (standard operating procedures), metrics reporting, or corporate dashboards. Be sure to have the project team pass along the materials that help facilitate this effort.

In Summary

That's it; we're done and dusted! In our Reflect leg, we can either close off this project completely or set up the next project and/or team for success. We learned how to use retrospectives in some new ways and drill down to the root cause. We set up our vendor and procurement processes for success in the future and finally, we celebrated our success!

Well done!

CHAPTER 6

Now What?

Well, we made it! I made it through all this writing, and you (perhaps) made it through all the reading! I wanted to wrap up with one last resource that gives you some guidance on where to start applying these techniques. You'll want to start in areas that demonstrate value and then build from there. Let's face it: It took me a 40-year career and at least 18 months to gather my thoughts and practice with all these techniques and you can't and won't and shouldn't apply them all at once!

Where to Start?

I'm a big fan of the saying, "If they don't get the question, don't shove the answer down their throats!" You need to decide where you are in your career and where your organization is at relative to project management and collaboration. It's a spectrum: think of it like in Figure 6.1.

As project managers, whether with the title or not, we can improve project practices and build collaboration by leading and learning within

Very disciplined PM practices

Command and control
Hierarchical organization

Values based
Psychologically safe
Collaborative organization

What's a project manager?
Why do we need one?

Figure 6.1 Where to start

our organization. Remember, you want to try and utilize some of these techniques to either increase collaboration in your organization or improve project structure.

So, figure out the landscape and then consider the scenarios in Figure 6.2.

Here are some suggestions based on what quadrant you find yourself and your project in.

Quadrant 1—Adding the Human Touch

This quadrant finds you in a corporate environment that is traditional and hierarchical and, at the same time, has disciplined or mature project management practices. I've found in this situation it's best to focus on adding the "softer" or more emotionally intelligent practices into your projects. These types of situations usually have hard skill tools and techniques firmly established particularly in the areas of time reporting, status reports, change request processes, time, budget, and scope management. Also they often have a Project Management Office that focuses on standardization of PM practices. They can benefit from improvement around facilitation skills, team pulse checks, and incorporating

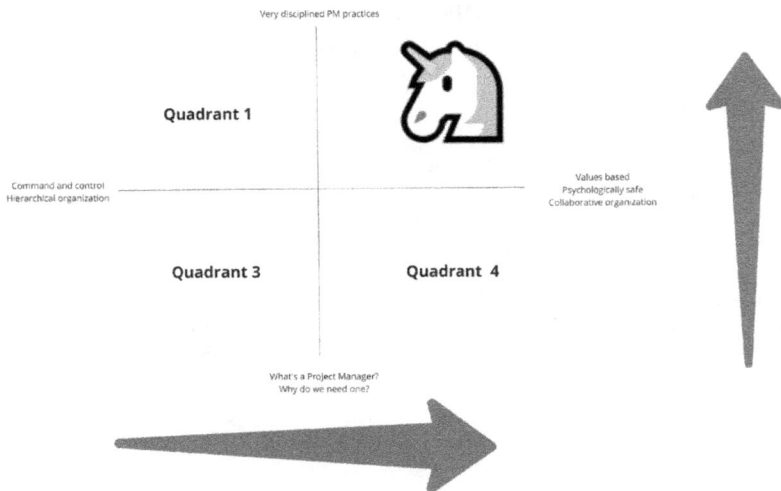

Figure 6.2 Change quadrants

feedback through retrospectives on the initiation (Listen) and planning (Understand) techniques. Also, these are the elements that AI can't replicate!

Table 6.1 has some suggestions specifically focused on adding the human touch.

Table 6.1 Quadrant 1—reference, tools, and techniques

Chapter	Reference, Tools, and Techniques
Chapter 2: Listen—Qualifying Our Ideas	• 1.4 Resource Strategy
Chapter 3: Understand—Planning for Success	• Project Team Kickoff—team norms • Go/No Go and Learn—team norms retrospective
Chapter 4: Create—Delivering Value	• Go/No Go and Learn—team norms retrospective

Chapter 5: Reflect—Learning and Celebrating	• 4.2 Retrospectives
	  ○ Retrospective on team culture
	  ○ Retrospective as therapy
	• 4.4 Off-Board Our Team
	• Celebrate Success

Quadrant 2—You're a Unicorn!

This is a magical place where there are robust project management practices, which in my books means not only doing the project right but doing the right project and is *also* a values-based psychologically safe workplace with amazing collaboration. If this is you, *please* give me a call; I'd love to meet you and share stories!

Quadrant 3—Improving Structure and Collaboration

In this quadrant, you're trying to balance improving project processes while not losing sight of the people part of projects. It's important to bring both aspects up to a higher level and not put too much emphasis on just one. That will mostly involve establishing a baseline to determine where these are at.

To determine the baseline, I recommend playing a game of PMGB: Run the board. Review your most recent project, run through the board and determine where things worked well and where there were gaps; then select some of the gaps to address in your next project. Pay particular attention to the major legs; often organizations are good at executing projects—the Create leg of the board—and can start improving project practices by working on selecting the right projects and/or planning them better; so look to the Listen and Understand legs.

Table 6.2 provides some suggestions specifically focused on improving structure and collaboration:

Table 6.2 Quadrant 3—reference, tools, and techniques

Chapter	Reference, Tools, and Techniques
Chapter 2: Listen—Qualifying Our Ideas	• Does this qualify as a project? • 1.3 Define Project Success • Go/No Go and Learn
Chapter 3: Understand—Planning for Success	• Project Team Kickoff • Collaborative Project Charter • Go/No Go and Learn—team norms
Chapter 4: Create—Delivering Value	• 3.4 Managing Change • 3.5 Making Decisions • Go/No Go and Learn—team norms
Chapter 5: Reflect—Learning and Celebrating	• 4.1 What's Next • 4.2 Retrospectives • 4.5 Celebrate Success

Quadrant 4—Bringing Order to Chaos

This quadrant is often characterized by what I describe as "good people make up for bad processes." The organization may be relatively new. I often find they have achieved their first million dollars of revenue and are now struggling to get to that $3 million to $5+ million mark. This often means there is enough staff that they need to get more discipline and standardization in their project processes but already have many cultural practices, rituals, and feedback systems in place. You don't want to upset or disrupt the cultural pieces; you do want to leverage them wherever possible in your project.

To start improving the project practices, you're looking to the basics of each leg—doing the right project as well as doing the project right. Some suggestions specifically focused on adding project structure are given in Table 6.3.

Table 6.3 Quadrant 4—reference, tools, and techniques

Chapter	Reference, Tools, and Techniques
Chapter 2: Listen—Qualifying Our Ideas	• Does this qualify as a project? • 1.3 Define Project Success • Go/No Go and Learn
Chapter 3: Understand—Planning for Success	• Project Team Kickoff • Collaborative Project Charter • 2.5 Communication • Go/No Go and Learn
Chapter 4: Create—Delivering Value	• 3.4 Managing Change • Go/No Go and Learn
Chapter 5: Reflect—Learning and Celebrating	• 4.1 What's Next • 4.2 Retrospectives • 4.3 Off-Board Vendors • 4.4 Off-Board People • Customer Sign-Off

You Can't Change Everything All at Once!

Last piece of advice before I'm done! Rome wasn't built in a day, and you can't change an organization overnight. Be cognizant of how much change an organization can absorb! This can be from the perspective of individual project team members, executives, project sponsors, and project customers. I've found that too many organizations are guilty of boiling the ocean—trying to do too much at once and doing none of it well or just never completing anything.

Remember in Chapter 1, Introduction, we talked about processes and projects and the difference? Remember the triangle (Figure 6.3).

You'll want to start out making your project processes effective: Start there, then do retrospectives as we described at the end of each leg,

Flexibility

Robust

Responsive   Resilient

Standardize   Customer

Streamline   Simplify   Corporate   Cost

Efficiency   **Effectiveness**

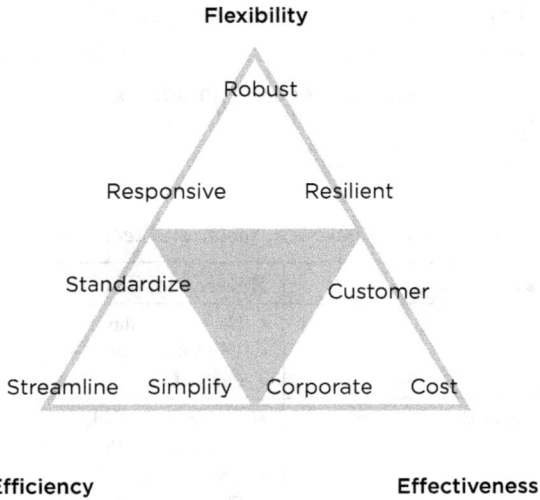

Figure 6.3 Where to focus change

and iterate by adding or improving either efficiency or flexibility. With the cultural and collaboration practices, keep the same thing in mind and utilize team pulse checks and retrospectives to determine your next steps—let your team be your guide!

The End

About the Author

Annie MacLeod has a real passion for ensuring that her clients are personally and professionally successful. She began her project management (PM) career in the tech sector and started her own consulting firm, Business Improvement Consulting Services Inc. (BICS), over 20 years ago. BICS specializes in making project teams and projects successful by streamlining PM practices and having highly effective project teams. More recently, she has added writing to her passions and is a regular contributor of articles for The Digital Project Manager community. She works with individual project managers and organizations to customize their PM practices and enhance them with digital collaboration techniques.

Finally, she is passionate about collaboration and has become an evangelist for Miro, the online collaboration product at the forefront of making meetings, projects, and learning truly effective in the remote world. With this passion, she is a Miro volunteer and participates in planning, facilitating, and providing expertise and is also a member of their expert community.

When she is not working, she pursues her passion of finding the best bakeries in the Okanagan and participates in any water activity available—sailing, stand-up paddleboard, or swimming.

Index

OTHER TITLES IN THE PORTFOLIO AND PROJECT MANAGEMENT COLLECTION

Kam Jugdev, Athabasca University, Editor

- *Power Skills That Lead to Exceptional Performance* by Neal Whitten
- *A Project Sponsor's Warp-Speed Guide* by Yogi Schulz and Jocelyn Lapointe
- *Great Meetings Build Great Teams* by Rich Maltzman and Jim Stewart
- *When Graduation's Over, Learning Begins* by Roger Forsgren
- *Project Control Methods and Best Practices* by Yakubu Olawale
- *Managing Projects With PMBOK 7* by James W. Marion and Tracey Richardson
- *Shields Up* by Gregory J. Skulmoski
- *Greatness in Construction History* by Sherif Hashem
- *The Inner Building Blocks* by Abhishek Rai
- *Project Profitability* by Reginald Tomas Lee
- *Moving the Needle With Lean OKRs* by Bart den Haak
- *Lean Knowledge Management* by Roger Forsgren

Concise and Applied Business Books

The Collection listed above is one of 30 business subject collections that Business Expert Press has grown to make BEP a premiere publisher of print and digital books. Our concise and applied books are for...

- Professionals and Practitioners
- Faculty who adopt our books for courses
- Librarians who know that BEP's Digital Libraries are a unique way to offer students ebooks to download, not restricted with any digital rights management
- Executive Training Course Leaders
- Business Seminar Organizers

Business Expert Press books are for anyone who needs to dig deeper on business ideas, goals, and solutions to everyday problems. Whether one print book, one ebook, or buying a digital library of 110 ebooks, we remain the affordable and smart way to be business smart. For more information, please visit www.businessexpertpress.com or contact sales@businessexpertpress.com.

www.ingramcontent.com/pod-product-compliance
Lightning Source LLC
Chambersburg PA
CBHW061315220326
41599CB00026B/4889